Betty Crocker's

Shortcut Cooking for the SmartCook

Betty Crocker's
Shortcut Cooking for the SmartCook

Prentice Hall

New York   London   Toronto   Sydney   Tokyo   Singapore

PRENTICE HALL GENERAL REFERENCE
15 Columbus Circle
New York, New York 10023

Library of Congress Cataloging-in-Publication data

    Crocker, Betty.
      [Shortcut cooking for the smartcook]
      Betty Crocker's shortcut cooking for the smartcook.
        p.   cm.
      Includes index.
      ISBN 0-13-067208-4 : $20.00
      1. Quick and easy cookery. I. Title. II. Title: Shortcut
    cooking for the smartcook.
    TX833.5.C76 1992
    641.5'12—dc20   91-40297
                                                  CIP

Manufactured in the United States of America

10 9 8 7 6 5 4 3 2 1

Originally published under the title *Betty Crocker's SmartCook*™

Introduction

We invite you to be a SmartCook. Whether you need recipes fast enough for family or fancy enough for friends, you'll find *SmartCook* has all the ingredients to make you the smartest cook around!

This indispensable collection of delicious, easy-to-prepare recipes based on fresh ingredients was created just for you. Knowing how important your time is, we've designed a cookbook with *you* in mind, including microwave directions, recipe variations, and beautiful photographs that provide simple but creative serving ideas.

More than just a cookbook, *SmartCook* should be part of your life-style. We've created two sections for how you prefer to cook. Our "Fix It Fast" section gives you no-fuss, no-nonsense favorites. Streamlined for success, these shortcut show-offs are ready from start to finish in 45 minutes or less. "Fix It and Forget It" is full of worry-free recipes that let you do the work first and then sit back and relax.

Each recipe has been kitchen-tested in the Betty Crocker kitchens—an assurance that these recipes have been created and chosen for your needs. With *SmartCook*, you'll find style and ease make perfect partners.

THE BETTY CROCKER EDITORS

Contents

Fix It Fast

Main-dish Salads

Fresh, little-cooking-required salads are a busy cook's saving grace. Starting with precooked meats or deli items, you can whip up these recipes or their variations in minutes. Arrange them attractively on salad plates and whisk them straight to the table.

Chicken and Fruit Salad with Green Chili Dressing

4 SERVINGS

3 cups bite-size pieces salad greens and shredded
   red cabbage
2 cups cut-up cooked chicken or turkey
1½ pounds honeydew, cantaloupe, casaba or
   Spanish melon, cut into thin wedges
2 cups bite-size pieces pineapple (about
   ½ medium)
½ small jicama, cut into julienne strips, or
   2 stalks celery, sliced
Green Chili Dressing (below)

Arrange salad greens and cabbage on platter or 4 salad plates; top with chicken, melon, pineapple and jicama. Garnish with lime slices and cilantro sprigs if desired. Serve with Green Chili Dressing.

GREEN CHILI DRESSING

1 cup mayonnaise or salad dressing
2 tablespoons lime juice
1 to 2 tablespoons finely chopped mild or hot
   green chilies
1 green onion (with top), thinly sliced, or
   2 tablespoons snipped cilantro

Mix all ingredients.

Chicken and Fruit Salad with Green Chili Dressing

German-style Hot Chicken Salad

4 boneless skinless chicken breast halves (about
   1 pound)
$1/4$ cup vegetable oil
1 tablespoon all-purpose flour
$1/4$ cup water
2 tablespoons white wine vinegar
2 teaspoons Dijon-style mustard
1 tablespoon snipped fresh thyme leaves or 1
   teaspoon dried thyme leaves
2 ounces mushrooms, sliced (about $3/4$ cup)
2 green onions (with tops), thinly sliced
Salt and pepper to taste
$1/2$ bunch romaine, torn into bite-size pieces
2 medium tomatoes, cut into wedges

Cook chicken breast halves in oil in 10-inch skillet over medium heat until done, about 6 minutes on each side. Remove chicken from skillet. Drain chicken; cool slightly. Cut into thin slices.

Stir flour into drippings in skillet. Cook over low heat, stirring constantly, until smooth and bubbly. Remove from heat; stir in water, vinegar, mustard, thyme, mushrooms and onions. Cook over low heat, stirring constantly, until mixture is bubbly. Cook and stir 1 minute. Sprinkle with salt and pepper.

Divide romaine among 4 salad plates. Arrange chicken and tomatoes on romaine; spoon mushroom mixture over top.

German-style Hot Chicken Salad with Cracklin's: Prepare as directed above except substitute 2 whole chicken breasts (about 2 pounds) for the boneless skinless chicken breast halves. Remove bones and skin from chicken, reserving skin. Heat oven to 375°. Place skin, fat sides down, in ungreased jelly roll pan, $15^{1/2}$ x $10^{1/2}$ x 1 inch; sprinkle with seasoned salt. Bake until crisp, about 20 minutes; drain. Cool; cut into small pieces. Sprinkle Chicken Cracklin's on salads.

German-style Hot Chicken Salad with Cracklin's

Wilted Spinach and Chicken Salad

1 boneless skinless whole chicken breast (about
   ½ pound)
4 slices bacon
1 tablespoon sesame seed
¼ cup vinegar
2 teaspoons sugar
1 teaspoon cornstarch
½ teaspoon salt
¼ teaspoon pepper
1 pound spinach
½ small red onion, thinly sliced

Cut chicken breast into 1-inch pieces; reserve. Cook bacon in 4-quart Dutch oven over medium heat until crisp. Drain bacon, reserving fat in Dutch oven; crumble bacon and reserve. Cook and stir chicken and sesame seed in bacon fat over medium heat until chicken is white, 6 to 7 minutes.

Mix vinegar, sugar, cornstarch, salt and pepper; stir into chicken mixture. Heat to boiling, stirring constantly. Stir 1 minute more. Remove from heat; add spinach and onion. Toss until spinach is wilted, 2 to 3 minutes; sprinkle with bacon. Serve immediately.

Basic Chicken Salad

½ cup mayonnaise or salad dressing
1 tablespoon lemon juice
½ teaspoon salt
¼ teaspoon pepper
2 cups cut-up cooked chicken or turkey
⅓ cup toasted slivered almonds or chopped nuts
2 medium stalks celery, sliced

Mix mayonnaise, lemon juice, salt and pepper in medium bowl; toss with chicken, almonds and celery. Serve on salad greens or as directed below if desired.

Fruited Chicken Salad: Stir 1 cup seedless grapes or 1 can (11 ounces) mandarin orange segments, drained, into salad just before serving.

Bacon Chicken Salad: Stir 4 slices bacon, crisply cooked and crumbled, into salad just before serving.

Chicken and Egg Salad: Stir 2 hard-cooked eggs, chopped, into salad.

Seafood Salad: Substitute 2 cups mixed cooked seafood (crabmeat, lobster, shrimp, scallops) for the chicken.

Tuna Salad: Decrease mayonnaise to ⅓ cup and salt to ¼ teaspoon. Substitute 2 cans (6½ ounces each) tuna, drained, for the chicken.

Chicken and Seafood Salads with Asparagus: Prepare Basic Chicken Salad and Seafood Salad. Line 6 salad plates with salad greens. Arrange chilled asparagus spears in spoke fashion on greens, dividing plate into thirds. Spoon 1 small serving each of Chicken Salad, Seafood Salad and deli macaroni salad between asparagus spears. Arrange chilled artichoke hearts, tomato wedges and pitted ripe olives on each plate.

Chicken Salad with Avocados: Prepare Basic Chicken Salad, Seafood Salad, or Tuna Salad. Peel and cut 2 avocados lengthwise into halves; remove pits. Place avocado halves, cut sides up, on salad plates; spoon about ½ cup salad over each. Or cut each half lengthwise into 6 or 7 slices and arrange in fan shape on salad plates; spoon about ½ cup salad next to avocado slices. Garnish with radishes.

Chicken Salad with Cantaloupe: Prepare Basic Chicken Salad, Fruited Chicken Salad or Seafood Salad. Cut 1 medium cantaloupe into 4 wedges; scoop out seeds. Spoon about ½ cup salad onto each melon wedge. Garnish with green onion slices if desired. Or cut cantaloupe into halves and each half into 6 slices; pare if desired. Line 4 salad plates with salad greens. Arrange 3 slices cantaloupe and about ½ cup salad on each. Arrange strawberries, banana slices or other fresh fruit on each plate if desired.

Chicken Salad in Pineapple Shells: Cut pineapple lengthwise into halves through green top; cut each half into halves. Cut core from each fourth and cut along curved edges of fruit with grapefruit knife; remove pineapple. Drain pineapple shells upside down. Cut up enough pineapple to measure 1 cup; use remaining pineapple as desired. Prepare Fruited Chicken Salad as directed except substitute 1 cup cut-up pineapple for the grapes. Spoon about ½ cup salad into each pineapple shell. Garnish with watercress if desired.

Following pages: Fruited Chicken Salad (right) and Turkey Salad with Honey Almonds

Turkey Salad with Honey Almonds

Creamy Honey Dressing (below)
½ cup honey-roasted almonds
8 ounces thinly sliced cooked turkey or chicken,
  cut into ¼-inch strips (about 2 cups)
4 ounces provolone or Swiss cheese, cut into
  cubes
2 medium stalks celery, sliced
2 unpared tart red apples, cut into cubes
Salad greens

Prepare Creamy Honey Dressing. Toss dressing and remaining ingredients except salad greens. Spoon onto salad greens; sprinkle with additional honey-roasted almonds if desired.

CREAMY HONEY DRESSING

½ cup dairy sour cream or plain yogurt
2 tablespoons honey
1 tablespoon snipped parsley or 1 teaspoon
  parsley flakes
1 teaspoon dry mustard
1 to 2 teaspoons lemon juice

Mix all ingredients in large bowl.

Italian Tuna and Spiral Pasta Salad

4 SERVINGS

1 package (7 ounces) uncooked spiral macaroni
   (about 3 cups)
2 cans (6½ ounces each) tuna, chilled and
   drained
1 jar (6 ounces) marinated artichoke hearts,
   chilled and undrained
¼ cup Italian dressing
2 tablespoons snipped parsley
2 tablespoons capers, drained
Dash of pepper

Cook macaroni as directed on package; drain. Rinse in cold water; drain. Mix macaroni and remaining ingredients. Serve on salad greens if desired.

Dilled Egg and Shrimp Salad

4 SERVINGS

⅓ cup mayonnaise or salad dressing
2 teaspoons snipped fresh dill weed or
   ½ teaspoon dried dill weed
1 teaspoon prepared mustard
½ teaspoon salt
¼ teaspoon pepper
6 hard-cooked eggs, chilled and coarsely chopped
2 stalks celery, sliced
2 green onions (with tops), sliced
1 package (6 ounces) frozen cooked shrimp,
   thawed
Lettuce leaves

Mix mayonnaise, dill, mustard, salt and pepper in large bowl until well blended. Gently stir in eggs, celery, onions and shrimp. Serve immediately on lettuce leaves or store in refrigerator.

Grilled Salmon Salad

4 small salmon steaks, each about 1 inch thick
  (about 1½ pounds)
1 tablespoon snipped fresh marjoram leaves or 1
  teaspoon dried marjoram leaves
½ teaspoon salt
¼ teaspoon pepper
½ cup oil-and-vinegar dressing
6 cups mixed salad greens
2 tablespoons capers, drained

Sprinkle salmon steaks with marjoram, salt and pepper. Set oven control to broil. Place salmon on rack in broiler pan; drizzle with 1 tablespoon of the dressing.

Broil salmon with tops about 3 inches from heat until opaque, 7 to 10 minutes. Turn; drizzle with 1 tablespoon dressing. Broil until salmon flakes easily with fork, about 5 minutes longer.

Mix salad greens and capers; toss with remaining dressing. Divide among 4 plates; top with salmon steaks.

Salmon and Grapefruit Salad

1 container (6 ounces) plain yogurt
1 tablespoon grated grapefruit peel
½ teaspoon salt
3 cups bite-size pieces salad greens
1 tablespoon tarragon vinegar
1 teaspoon seasoned salt
2 stalks celery, cut into thin diagonal slices
1 grapefruit, pared and sectioned
1 can (16 ounces) salmon, drained and flaked

Mix yogurt, grapefruit peel and salt; cover and refrigerate. Just before serving, toss remaining ingredients. Serve with dressing and, if desired, on salad greens.

Grilled Salmon Salad

Seafood Pasta Salad with Ginger Dressing

8 ounces uncooked vermicelli
Ginger Dressing (below)
2 cups bite-size pieces cooked seafood or 1
  package (8 ounces) frozen salad-style
  imitation crabmeat, thawed
1/2 cup coarsely chopped jicama or water
  chestnuts
1/4 cup snipped cilantro or parsley
2 medium carrots, shredded
1 medium cucumber, halved and sliced

Break vermicelli into halves. Cook as directed on package; drain. Rinse in cold water; drain.

Prepare Ginger Dressing. Toss dressing, vermicelli and remaining ingredients. Spoon onto salad greens if desired.

GINGER DRESSING

1/3 cup mayonnaise or salad dressing
1/3 cup plain yogurt
1 tablespoon soy sauce
1 teaspoon sugar
1/2 teaspoon ground ginger
Dash of red pepper sauce, hot chili oil or hot
  sesame oil

Mix all ingredients in large bowl.

Chicken Pasta Salad with Ginger Dressing: Substitute 2 cups cut-up cooked chicken or turkey for the seafood.

Seafood Pasta Salad with Ginger Dressing

Warm Pork and Bulgur Salad with Apricots

1 small onion, chopped
2 tablespoons margarine or butter
1 can (10¾ ounces) condensed chicken broth
½ broth can water
1 cup uncooked bulgur
½ teaspoon salt
2 cups bite-size pieces cooked pork
½ cup snipped dried apricots
¼ cup oil-and-vinegar dressing
2 stalks celery, sliced
Salad greens

Cook and stir onion in margarine in 3-quart sauce-pan until tender. Add broth, water, bulgur and salt. Heat to boiling; reduce heat.

Cover and simmer 15 minutes. Remove from heat; stir in pork, apricots, dressing and celery. Spoon onto salad greens.

Chilled Pork and Bulgur Salad: Cover and refrigerate at least 2 hours. Just before serving, stir in 2 tablespoons additional oil-and-vinegar dressing.

Winter Fruit Salad with Ham and Walnuts

¼ cup dairy sour cream
¼ cup mayonnaise or salad dressing
½ teaspoon ground ginger
2 cups cut-up fully cooked smoked ham
½ cup snipped dates (about 3 ounces)
½ cup walnut pieces
2 medium unpared eating apples, cut into
    wedges
2 medium oranges, pared, cut into halves and
    sliced
1 package (6 ounces) shredded Swiss cheese
    (about 1½ cups)
Salad greens

Mix sour cream, mayonnaise and ginger in large bowl. Toss with remaining ingredients except salad greens. Serve on salad greens.

Prosciutto Salad with Grapefruit-Honey Dressing

4 SERVINGS

2 grapefruit
Grapefruit-Honey Dressing (below)
1/2 pound prosciutto or thinly sliced fully cooked
  smoked ham
Salad greens
3 unpared eating apples, sliced

Pare and section grapefruit, allowing juice to drain into bowl. Reserve 1/4 cup of the juice for Grapefruit-Honey Dressing; prepare dressing. Roll up prosciutto.

Arrange salad greens on platter or 4 salad plates. Arrange grapefruit, apples and prosciutto on greens. Serve with dressing.

GRAPEFRUIT-HONEY DRESSING

1/4 cup reserved grapefruit juice
3 tablespoons honey
3 tablespoons vegetable oil or dairy sour cream
1/4 teaspoon celery seed

Shake all ingredients in tightly covered container. Shake before using.

Following pages: Four presentations of Prosciutto Salad with Grapefruit-Honey Dressing

MAIN-DISH SALADS

Bacon and Tomato Salad

4 SERVINGS

Cucumber Yogurt Dressing (below)
Salad greens
6 plum tomatoes, sliced, or 3 medium tomatoes,
 cut into wedges
1 pound bacon, crisply cooked and crumbled
1 cup plain or seasoned croutons

Prepare Cucumber Yogurt Dressing. Arrange salad greens, tomatoes and bacon on 4 salad plates; sprinkle with croutons. Serve with dressing.

CUCUMBER YOGURT DRESSING

1 cup plain yogurt
½ cup chopped cucumber
1½ teaspoons sugar
1 teaspoon prepared horseradish
½ teaspoon salt
1 green onion, thinly sliced

Mix all ingredients. Cover and refrigerate until ready to serve.

Chicken, Bacon and Tomato Salad: Substitute 2 cups cut-up cooked chicken for ½ pound of the bacon.

Melon Salad with Pastrami and Cheese

4 SERVINGS

Salad greens
½ pound thinly sliced pastrami, cooked corned
 beef or fully cooked smoked ham
4 ounces caraway cheese or dilled Havarti
 cheese, cut into thin 2-inch strips
1 cantaloupe, casaba or honeydew melon (about
 3 pounds), pared and cut into 1-inch wedges
1 cucumber, cut into thin 2-inch strips*
Russian or creamy herb vinaigrette dressing

Arrange salad greens on platter or 4 salad plates. Arrange remaining ingredients except dressing on greens. Serve with dressing.

✱ 6 ounces fresh Chinese pea pods or sugar snap peas, cooked and drained, can be substituted for the cucumber.

Bacon and Tomato Salad

Ham Salad with Cheddar Dressing

3 cups bite-size pieces salad greens
1½ cups frozen green peas, thawed and drained
¾ pound fully cooked smoked ham, cut into ½-inch cubes (about 2 cups)
½ head cauliflower, broken into flowerets
½ small red onion, thinly sliced
Cheddar Dressing (below)

Toss all ingredients except Cheddar Dressing. Serve with dressing and freshly ground pepper if desired.

CHEDDAR DRESSING

1 cup shredded Cheddar cheese (4 ounces)
¼ cup milk
2 tablespoons wine vinegar
¼ teaspoon salt
1 package (3 ounces) cream cheese, softened
1 clove garlic

Place all ingredients in workbowl of food processor fitted with steel blade or in blender container. Cover and process, stopping once to scrape down sides, until mixture is of uniform consistency, about 30 seconds.

Minted Cottage Cheese Salad with Fruit

1 container (16 ounces) small curd creamed
   cottage cheese
1 tablespoon snipped fresh mint leaves
Lettuce leaves
1 cup blueberries, raspberries or blackberries
1/2 pint medium strawberries (about 1 cup) or 1
   large peach or nectarine, sliced
2 medium bananas, sliced
Coarsely chopped salted or toasted nuts
Ginger-Honey Dressing (below)

Mix cottage cheese and mint. Divide lettuce leaves among 4 salad plates. Spoon cheese mixture onto each. Arrange fruit on top; sprinkle with nuts. Serve with Ginger-Honey Dressing.

GINGER-HONEY DRESSING

1/4 cup vegetable oil
1/4 cup lime juice
1/4 cup honey
2 tablespoons mayonnaise or salad dressing
1/4 teaspoon salt
1/4 teaspoon ground ginger

Shake all ingredients in tightly covered container.

Following pages: Minted Cottage Cheese Salad with Fruit

Greek Salad

1 medium head lettuce, torn into bite-size pieces
1 bunch romaine, torn into bite-size pieces
24 Greek or green olives
10 radishes, sliced
1 medium cucumber, sliced
1 bunch green onions (with tops), cut into ½-inch pieces
1 cup crumbled feta or chèvre cheese (about 4 ounces)
1 carrot, shredded
Vinegar Dressing (below)

Toss lettuce and romaine. Arrange remaining ingredients except Vinegar Dressing on top. Serve with dressing.

VINEGAR DRESSING

½ cup olive or vegetable oil
⅓ cup wine vinegar
1 tablespoon snipped fresh oregano leaves or 1 teaspoon dried oregano leaves
1 teaspoon salt

Shake all ingredients in tightly covered container.

Greek Salad

MAIN-DISH SALADS

27

Hearty Soups

Who'd have thought you could have real homemade flavor in thirty minutes? The secret lies in using canned soup or broth, bottled clam juice or vegetable juice as a basic stock and then adding meat, fresh vegetables and flavorful herbs. A bonus: Many of these recipes are as delicious cold as they are hot.

Minestrone with Pesto

6 SERVINGS

4 cups raw vegetable pieces*
2 ounces uncooked spaghetti, broken into 2- to
   3-inch pieces, or ½ cup uncooked macaroni
½ teaspoon dried basil leaves
⅛ teaspoon pepper
1 medium onion, chopped
1 clove garlic, finely chopped
1 can (15 ounces) kidney or garbanzo beans,
   undrained
2 cans (10½ ounces each) condensed beef broth
2 broth cans water
5 ounces spinach, cut crosswise into ¼-inch
   strips
Pesto (page 144) or prepared pesto

Heat all ingredients except spinach and Pesto to boiling in 4-quart Dutch oven; reduce heat.

Cover and simmer until vegetables and spaghetti are tender, about 10 minutes. Stir in spinach until wilted. Serve with Pesto and, if desired, grated Parmesan cheese.

✱ Sliced carrots, celery, zucchini or yellow summer squash, green or yellow beans, cut into 1-inch slices, chopped tomatoes or shelled peas can be used.

Minestrone with Pesto

Oriental-style Chicken Noodle Soup

3 cups water
1 package (3 ounces) chicken flavor Oriental-style 3-minute noodles
2 cups cut-up cooked chicken
2 medium stalks bok choy (with leaves), cut into ¼-inch slices
1 medium carrot, sliced
1 teaspoon sesame oil, if desired

Heat water to boiling in 3-quart saucepan. Break apart block of noodles into water; stir in chicken, bok choy and carrot.

Heat to boiling; reduce heat. Simmer uncovered 3 minutes, stirring occasionally. Stir in Flavor Packet and sesame oil.

Hot-and-Sour Fish Soup

4 SERVINGS

2 tablespoons cornstarch
2 tablespoons cold water
½ pound fish fillets, cut into 1-inch pieces
3 tablespoons white vinegar
2 teaspoons soy sauce
2 medium carrots, cut into thin strips
2 bottles (8 ounces each) clam juice or 2 cups fish or chicken broth
1 jar (7 ounces) sliced shiitake mushrooms, undrained
1 to 2 teaspoons red pepper sauce
4 ounces fresh Chinese pea pods or 1 package (6 ounces) frozen Chinese pea pods, thawed

Mix cornstarch and cold water. Mix cornstarch mixture and remaining ingredients except pepper sauce and pea pods in 4-quart Dutch oven. Heat to boiling; reduce heat.

Cover and simmer until fish flakes easily with fork, 3 to 5 minutes. Stir in pepper sauce and pea pods.

TO MICROWAVE: Decrease vinegar to 2 tablespoons and use 1 teaspoon red pepper sauce. Coarsely shred carrots. Mix fish, vinegar, soy sauce, carrots, clam juice and mushrooms in 3-quart microwavable casserole. Cover tightly and microwave on high (100%) 5 minutes.

Mix cornstarch and cold water; stir into fish mixture. Cover tightly and microwave, stirring every 2 minutes, until mixture thickens and boils, 8 to 10 minutes. Stir in pepper sauce and pea pods. Cover tightly and microwave until pea pods are hot, 1 to 2 minutes.

Hot-and-Sour Fish Soup (top) and Oriental-style Chicken Noodle Soup

Oyster and Vegetable Chowder

1/3 cup margarine or butter
1 1/2 pints shucked select or large oysters,
    undrained*
1 package (16 ounces) frozen corn-broccoli
    mixture
3 1/2 cups milk
1 1/2 teaspoons salt
Dash of pepper

Heat margarine in 3-quart saucepan until melted. Stir in oysters and vegetables. Cook over medium heat, stirring frequently, until edges of oysters are curled and vegetables are done, about 14 minutes.

Stir in milk, salt and pepper. Cook over low heat, stirring frequently, until hot.

✱ 3 cans (8 ounces each) whole oysters, undrained, can be substituted for fresh oysters; stir in with the milk.

Chicken and Broccoli Chowder

2 cups water
1/3 cup chopped onion
2 teaspoons instant chicken bouillon
1 package (10 ounces) frozen chopped broccoli
1 1/3 cups mashed potato mix (dry)
2 cups cut-up cooked chicken
2 cups shredded Swiss cheese (8 ounces)
2 cups milk
1/2 teaspoon salt

Heat water, onion, bouillon (dry) and broccoli to boiling in 3-quart saucepan; reduce heat. Cover and simmer 5 minutes.

Stir in potato mix until well blended; stir in remaining ingredients. Heat over low heat, stirring occasionally, until hot and cheese is melted, about 5 minutes.

Oyster and Vegetable Chowder

Fish and Corn Chowder

6 slices bacon, cut into ½-inch pieces
2 cups water
1 teaspoon salt
¼ teaspoon white pepper
1 pound cod, cut into 1-inch pieces
4 new potatoes, cut into ¼-inch slices
2 medium stalks celery, sliced
1 medium onion, chopped
1 can (17 ounces) whole kernel corn, undrained
1 cup half-and-half

Cook bacon in 4-quart Dutch oven until crisp; remove bacon and drain. Drain fat from Dutch oven.

Stir remaining ingredients except half-and-half into Dutch oven. Heat to boiling; reduce heat. Cover and simmer until fish and potatoes are done, 15 to 20 minutes. Stir in half-and-half; heat until hot. Sprinkle each serving with bacon and, if desired, garnish with celery leaves.

Dilled Salmon Chowder

2 medium potatoes, cut into ½-inch cubes
2 medium stalks celery, sliced
1 medium carrot, sliced
1 medium onion, chopped
1 can (10¾ ounces) condensed chicken broth
1 broth can water
1 tablespoon snipped fresh dill weed or 1
    teaspoon dried dill weed
½ teaspoon salt
¼ teaspoon pepper
2 cups half-and-half
1 can (15½ ounces) salmon, drained and flaked

Heat to boiling all ingredients except half-and-half and salmon in 4-quart Dutch oven; reduce heat.

Cover and simmer until vegetables are crisp-tender, about 10 minutes. Stir in half-and-half and salmon; heat until hot.

TO MICROWAVE: Mix all ingredients except half-and-half and salmon in 3-quart microwavable casserole. Cover tightly and microwave on high (100%) 8 minutes; stir.

Cover tightly and microwave until vegetables are crisp-tender, 8 to 10 minutes longer. Stir in half-and-half and salmon. Cover tightly and microwave, stirring every 2 minutes, until hot, 4 to 5 minutes.

Beans and Franks Soup

3 carrots, sliced
2 medium onions, chopped
1 clove garlic, finely chopped
2 tablespoons margarine or butter
1 can (28 ounces) baked beans in brown sugar
    sauce
1 can (12 ounces) vegetable juice or tomato juice
6 frankfurters, cut into 1-inch slices
1 teaspoon Worcestershire sauce
Shredded American or Cheddar cheese

Cook carrots, onions and garlic in margarine in 3-quart saucepan, stirring frequently, until carrots are crisp-tender.

Stir in remaining ingredients except cheese. Heat over medium heat, stirring occasionally, until hot. Sprinkle with cheese.

Beans and Franks Soup with Vegetables: Prepare as directed above except omit carrots. Stir in 1 package (10 ounces) frozen mixed vegetables with the beans.

Southwestern Bean Soup with Chilies

1 medium onion, sliced
1 large clove garlic, crushed
2 tablespoons margarine or butter
1 can (28 ounces) whole tomatoes, undrained
1 can (20 ounces) kidney beans, drained
1 can (16 ounces) pinto beans, drained
1 can (4 ounces) chopped green chilies, drained
1 tablespoon chili powder
1/4 teaspoon ground coriander
1/2 cup shredded Cheddar cheese (2 ounces)
1 cup shredded Monterey Jack cheese (4 ounces)

Cook and stir onion and garlic in margarine in 3-quart saucepan over medium heat until onion is tender, about 5 minutes. Stir in remaining ingredients except cheeses; break up tomatoes. Heat to boiling; reduce heat. Cover and simmer 30 minutes.

Stir in Cheddar cheese and 1/2 cup of the Monterey Jack cheese; heat over low heat, stirring occasionally, just until cheese is melted. Sprinkle each serving with remaining Monterey Jack cheese.

TO MICROWAVE: Place onion, garlic and margarine in 3-quart microwavable casserole. Cover tightly and microwave on high (100%) until onion is tender, 2 to 4 minutes. Stir in remaining ingredients except cheeses; break up tomatoes. Cover tightly and microwave 10 minutes; stir.

Cover tightly and microwave until hot and bubbly, 6 to 9 minutes longer. Stir in Cheddar cheese and 1/2 cup of the Monterey Jack cheese. Cover tightly and let stand until cheese is melted, about 5 minutes. Sprinkle each serving with remaining Monterey Jack cheese.

Tortellini and Sausage Soup

1 pound bulk Italian sausage
1 medium onion, coarsely chopped
3 cups water
1/2 teaspoon dried basil leaves
1/2 teaspoon dried oregano leaves
2 carrots, sliced
1 medium zucchini or yellow summer squash,
   halved and sliced
2 cans (10¾ ounces each) condensed tomato
   soup
8 ounces uncooked dried or frozen cheese- or
   meat-filled tortellini (2 cups)
Grated Parmesan cheese

Cook and stir sausage and onion in 4-quart Dutch oven until sausage is light brown; drain. Stir in remaining ingredients except cheese.

Heat to boiling; reduce heat. Cover and simmer until vegetables and tortellini are tender, about 20 minutes. Serve with cheese.

Garbanzo Bean and Sausage Soup: Use 1 can (15 ounces) garbanzo beans, drained, for the tortellini.

French Cabbage Soup

3½ cups water
2 tablespoons margarine or butter
1 tablespoon instant chicken bouillon (dry)
1 teaspoon Worcestershire sauce
1/4 teaspoon pepper
2 medium onions, thinly sliced
2 medium carrots, shredded
1 small head green cabbage, shredded
1 clove garlic, finely chopped
6 slices French bread, toasted
1½ cups shredded Swiss cheese (6 ounces)
1/4 cup grated Parmesan cheese

Heat all ingredients except bread and cheeses to boiling in 4-quart Dutch oven; reduce heat. Simmer uncovered, stirring occasionally, until vegetables are crisp-tender, 15 to 20 minutes.

Set oven control to broil. Pour soup into 6 oven-proof soup bowls or casseroles. Top each with 1 slice toast; sprinkle with Swiss and Parmesan cheeses. Broil soup with tops 3 to 4 inches from heat until cheese is melted and light brown, 1 to 2 minutes.

Tortellini and Sausage Soup

Tomato Vegetable Soup with Yogurt

1 can (24 ounces) tomato juice (3 cups)
¼ to ½ teaspoon ground red pepper
¼ teaspoon salt
1 package (10 ounces) frozen whole kernel corn
1 bunch green onions (about 6 with tops), sliced
1 medium red or green pepper, coarsely chopped
1 medium zucchini, coarsely chopped
1 container (18 ounces) plain yogurt

Heat all ingredients except yogurt to boiling in 4-quart Dutch oven; reduce heat. Simmer uncovered, stirring occasionally, until vegetables are crisp-tender, 7 to 8 minutes. Remove from heat; cool 5 minutes before adding yogurt to prevent curdling.

Stir yogurt into soup until smooth. Heat over medium heat, stirring constantly, just until hot (do not boil). Garnish with snipped cilantro or parsley if desired.

Cold Tomato Vegetable Soup with Yogurt: After stirring in yogurt, cover and refrigerate soup until chilled. Garnish with alfalfa sprouts if desired.

Green Pea Soup

1 package (16 ounces) frozen green peas
1 cup milk
2 tablespoons margarine or butter
2 tablespoons all-purpose flour
¾ teaspoon salt
⅛ teaspoon pepper
½ cup whipping cream or half-and-half
Mint leaves

Cook peas as directed on package; reserve ½ cup for garnish if desired. Place remaining peas and the milk in workbowl of food processor fitted with steel blade or in blender container. Cover and process until of uniform consistency.

Heat margarine in 2-quart saucepan until melted. Stir in flour, salt and pepper. Cook, stirring constantly, until smooth and bubbly. Remove from heat; stir in pea mixture. Heat to boiling, stirring constantly. Boil and stir 1 minute. Stir in cream; heat just until hot (do not boil). Garnish each serving with reserved peas and mint leaves if desired.

Cold Green Pea Soup: After stirring in cream, cover and refrigerate soup until chilled. If soup is too thick when ready to serve, stir in additional cream or half-and-half until of desired consistency.

Green Pea Soup with Ham: Prepare as directed above except process all of the peas. Substitute dash of ground ginger for the mint leaves. Garnish with ¼-inch strips fully cooked smoked ham.

Green Pea Soup with Smoked Fish: Prepare as directed above except process all of the peas. Substitute snipped fresh dill weed for the mint leaves. Garnish with small pieces of smoked fish.

TO MICROWAVE: Microwave peas in 1½-quart microwavable casserole as directed on package; drain. Continue as directed except place margarine in casserole. Cover with waxed paper and microwave on high (100%) until melted, 30 to 60 seconds. Stir in flour, salt and pepper; stir in pea mixture. Cover with waxed paper and microwave 1 minute; stir.

Cover with waxed paper and microwave to boiling, stirring every minute, 4 to 5 minutes; stir in cream. Cover with waxed paper and microwave just until hot, 30 to 60 seconds (do not boil). Garnish each serving with reserved peas and mint leaves.

HEARTY SOUPS

Cream of Carrot Soup

1 small onion, chopped
2 tablespoons margarine or butter
6 carrots, chopped
2 tablespoons dry white wine
3 cups water
1 tablespoon instant chicken bouillon
1 teaspoon salt
1/8 teaspoon ground nutmeg
Dash of pepper
1 cup whipping cream

Cook and stir onion in margarine in 2-quart saucepan until tender. Stir in carrots and wine. Heat to boiling; reduce heat. Cover and simmer 10 minutes. Stir in water, bouillon (dry), salt, nutmeg and pepper. Heat to boiling; reduce heat. Cover and simmer until carrots are tender, about 30 minutes.

Pour half the carrot mixture into blender container. Cover and blend on medium speed until smooth; strain. Repeat with remaining mixture. Heat until hot. Beat whipping cream until stiff; stir into soup.

Cream of Carrot Soup with Peas: Cook 1 cup frozen green peas as directed on package. Top each serving with 2 heaping tablespoonfuls peas.

TO MICROWAVE: Place onion and margarine in 2-quart microwavable casserole. Cover tightly and microwave on high (100%) until onion is tender, 2 to 3 minutes. Stir in carrots and wine. Cover tightly and microwave until carrots are tender, 7 to 10 minutes. Spoon carrot mixture into blender container; add 1 cup of the water. Cover and blend on medium speed until smooth.

Mix carrot mixture, remaining water, the bouillon (dry), salt, nutmeg and pepper in casserole. Cover tightly and microwave until hot and bubbly, 6 to 10 minutes. Beat whipping cream until stiff; stir into soup.

Green Pea Soup (top) and Cream of Carrot Soup

HEARTY SOUPS

Eggs and Cheese

Whether it's rich Asparagus and Eggs Mornay for brunch or a savory Mexican Omelet for dinner, egg dishes are invariably a hit. Often combined with cheese in unusual ways, as in Baked Apple and Cheese Pancake, these recipes are as wonderful for entertaining as they are for an impromptu supper.

Rolled Ham and Gruyère Omelet

6 SERVINGS

½ cup all-purpose flour
1 cup milk
2 tablespoons margarine or butter, melted
½ teaspoon salt
4 eggs
1 cup coarsely chopped fully cooked smoked ham
1 small onion, chopped
1½ cups shredded Gruyère or Swiss cheese (6 ounces)
1 cup chopped fresh spinach

Heat oven to 350°. Line jelly roll pan, 15½ x 10½ x 1 inch, with aluminum foil. Generously grease foil. Beat flour, milk, margarine, salt and eggs until well blended; pour into pan. Sprinkle with ham and onion.

Bake until eggs are set, 15 to 18 minutes. Immediately sprinkle with cheese and spinach; roll up, beginning at narrow end and using foil to lift and roll omelet. Arrange additional spinach leaves on serving plate if desired. Cut omelet into about 1½-inch slices.

Rolled Bacon and Gruyère Omelet: Substitute 8 slices bacon, crisply cooked and crumbled, for the ham.

Rolled Sausage and Gruyère Omelet: Substitute 1 package (8 ounces) fully cooked sausage links, cut up, for the ham.

Rolled Ham and Gruyère Omelet

43

Asparagus and Eggs Mornay

1½ pounds fresh asparagus
Mornay Sauce (below)
6 hard-cooked eggs, cut into fourths

Arrange asparagus spears crosswise in ungreased rectangular baking dish, 12 x 7½ x 2 inches. Cover with aluminum foil and bake in 400° oven until tender, about 20 minutes.

Prepare Mornay Sauce. Set oven control to broil. Arrange eggs on asparagus; spoon warm sauce over eggs. Broil with top about 4 inches from heat until sauce bubbles and browns slightly, 2 to 3 minutes.

MORNAY SAUCE

2 tablespoons margarine or butter
2 tablespoons all-purpose flour
¼ teaspoon salt
Dash of ground nutmeg
1¼ cups milk
¾ cup shredded Gruyère or Swiss cheese (3 ounces)
¼ cup grated Parmesan cheese

Heat margarine in 1½-quart saucepan over low heat until melted. Stir in flour, salt and nutmeg. Cook over low heat, stirring constantly, until smooth and bubbly. Remove from heat; stir in milk. Heat to boiling over medium heat, stirring constantly. Boil and stir 1 minute. Add cheeses; stir until melted.

TO MICROWAVE: Arrange asparagus spears crosswise in rectangular microwavable dish, 12 x 7½ x 2 inches. Cover with vented plastic wrap and microwave on high (100%) 4 minutes; rotate dish ½ turn. Microwave until stalk ends are just tender, 3 to 4 minutes longer; drain. Let stand covered.

To prepare Mornay Sauce: Place margarine in 4-cup microwavable measure. Microwave on high (100%) until melted, about 30 seconds. Stir in flour, salt and nutmeg until smooth. Gradually stir in milk. Microwave uncovered to boiling, 3 to 4 minutes, stirring every minute. Stir in cheeses until melted. Arrange eggs on asparagus. Pour hot sauce over eggs and asparagus. If desired, broil as directed above.

Asparagus and Eggs Mornay

Creamed Tarragon Eggs

1 can (10¾ ounces) condensed cream of celery
    soup
½ soup can milk
1 cup cooked green peas
1 teaspoon snipped fresh tarragon leaves or ½
    teaspoon dried tarragon leaves
6 hard-cooked eggs, cut into fourths
Shoestring potatoes, chow mein noodles or toast

Mix soup, milk, peas and tarragon in 2-quart sauce-pan. Heat to boiling over medium heat, stirring frequently. Carefully stir in eggs. Serve over shoestring potatoes.

TO MICROWAVE: Mix soup, milk, peas and tarragon in 2-quart microwavable casserole. Cover tightly and microwave on high (100%), stirring every 2 minutes, until hot and bubbly, 6 to 8 minutes. Carefully stir in eggs. Serve over shoestring potatoes.

Vegetable and Ham Omelet

1 package (12 ounces) loose-pack frozen hash
    brown potatoes
¼ cup vegetable oil
1 package (4 ounces) sliced fully cooked smoked
    ham, cut into ½-inch strips
1 medium onion, chopped
6 eggs
½ teaspoon salt
⅛ teaspoon pepper
1 cup frozen whole kernel corn *
2 tablespoons margarine or butter
Grated Parmesan cheese

Cook and stir potatoes in oil in 10-inch skillet over medium heat until tender, about 5 minutes. Stir in ham and onion. Cook, stirring occasionally, until onion is tender, about 5 minutes.

Beat eggs, salt and pepper. Stir corn and margarine into ham mixture; pour eggs over top. Cover and cook over medium-low heat until eggs are set and light brown on bottom, about 10 minutes. Sprinkle with cheese; cut into wedges.

✱ 1 can (8 ounces) whole kernel corn, drained, can be substituted for the 1 cup frozen corn.

Mexican Omelet

3 eggs
1 tablespoon margarine or butter
2 tablespoons chopped canned green chilies
¼ cup shredded Monterey Jack cheese (1 ounce)
Mexican salsa
Dairy sour cream

Mix eggs with fork just until whites and yolks are blended. Heat margarine in 8-inch skillet or omelet pan over medium-high heat just until margarine begins to brown. As margarine melts, tilt skillet to coat bottom completely.

Quickly pour eggs, all at once, into skillet. Slide skillet back and forth rapidly over heat and, at the same time, stir quickly with fork to spread eggs continuously over bottom of skillet as they thicken. Let stand over heat a few seconds to lightly brown bottom of omelet. (Do not overcook—omelet will continue to cook after folding.)

Tilt skillet; run fork under edge of omelet, then jerk skillet sharply to loosen eggs from bottom of skillet. Sprinkle with green chilies and cheese. Fold portion of omelet nearest you just to center. (Allow for portion of omelet to slide up side of skillet.)

Grasp skillet handle; turn omelet onto warm plate, flipping folded portion of omelet over so far side is on bottom. Tuck sides of omelet under if necessary. Top with salsa and sour cream; sprinkle with snipped cilantro if desired.

Blue Cheese Omelet with Pears

4 eggs
1 tablespoon margarine or butter
¼ cup crumbled Danish blue cheese or
   Gorgonzola cheese
1 tablespoon snipped chives
1 unpared pear, cut into wedges

Mix eggs with fork just until whites and yolks are blended. Heat margarine in 8-inch skillet or omelet pan over medium-high heat just until margarine begins to brown. As margarine melts, tilt skillet to coat bottom completely.

Quickly pour eggs, all at once, into skillet. Slide skillet back and forth rapidly over heat and, at the same time, stir quickly with fork to spread eggs continuously over bottom of pan as they thicken. Let stand over heat a few seconds to lightly brown bottom of omelet. (Do not overcook—omelet will continue to cook after folding.)

Tilt skillet; run fork under edge of omelet, then jerk skillet sharply to loosen eggs from bottom of skillet. Sprinkle with blue cheese and chives. Fold portion of omelet nearest you just to center. (Allow for portion of omelet to slide up side of skillet.)

Grasp skillet handle; turn omelet onto warm plate, flipping folded portion of omelet over so far side is on bottom. Serve with pear wedges.

Blue Cheese Omelet with Pears

Broccoli and Swiss Cheese Frittata

6 SERVINGS

1 medium onion, chopped
2 cloves garlic, finely chopped
2 tablespoons margarine or butter
1 tablespoon olive or vegetable oil
1 package (10 ounces) frozen chopped broccoli,
    thawed and drained
8 eggs
1/2 teaspoon salt
1/4 teaspoon pepper
1 cup shredded Swiss cheese (4 ounces)
1 to 2 tablespoons snipped fresh oregano leaves
    or 1 teaspoon dried oregano leaves
2 tablespoons shredded Swiss cheese

Cook onion and garlic in margarine and oil in 10-inch ovenproof skillet over medium heat, stirring frequently, until onion is tender, about 5 minutes. Remove from heat; stir in broccoli.

Beat eggs, salt and pepper until blended; stir in 1 cup cheese and the oregano. Pour over broccoli mixture. Cover and cook over medium-low heat until eggs are set around edge and light brown on bottom, 9 to 11 minutes.

Set oven control to broil. Broil frittata with top about 5 inches from heat until golden brown, about 2 minutes. Sprinkle with 2 tablespoons cheese; cut into wedges.

Crabmeat Frittata

6 SERVINGS

4 ounces mushrooms, sliced, or 1 jar (4 ounces)
    sliced mushrooms, drained
1 bunch green onions (with tops), sliced
1/4 cup margarine or butter
1 package (6 ounces) frozen crabmeat, thawed
    and drained
8 eggs
1/2 teaspoon lemon and pepper seasoning salt
1 cup shredded Fontina or Monterey Jack cheese
    (4 ounces)
1 tablespoon snipped fresh basil leaves or 1
    teaspoon dried basil leaves
2 tablespoons grated Parmesan cheese

Cook mushrooms and onions in margarine in 10-inch ovenproof skillet, stirring frequently, until tender, about 10 minutes. Stir in crabmeat.

Beat eggs and seasoning salt until blended; stir in Fontina cheese and basil. Pour over crabmeat mixture. Cover and cook over medium-low heat until eggs are set and light brown on bottom, 8 to 10 minutes.

Set oven control to broil. Broil frittata with top about 5 inches from heat until golden brown, about 2 minutes. Sprinkle with Parmesan cheese; cut into wedges.

Tex-Mex Scrambled Eggs with Tortillas

6 corn tortillas (about 6 inches in diameter)
3 tablespoons vegetable oil
1 bunch green onions (with tops), chopped
6 eggs, beaten
1 cup cubed Mexican-style process cheese spread
   with jalapeño chilies (about 4 ounces)
Chopped tomato

Cut each tortilla into 12 wedges. Heat oil in 10-inch skillet just until hot. Cook tortilla wedges in oil over medium-high heat, stirring frequently, until crisp; reduce heat. Add onions; cook and stir over medium heat 1 minute.

Pour eggs over tortilla mixture. As eggs begin to set at bottom and side, gently lift cooked portions with spatula so that thin, uncooked portion can flow to bottom. Do not stir.

Sprinkle with cheese; continue cooking until cheese is melted and eggs are thickened throughout but still moist, 1 to 2 minutes. Serve with tomato; sprinkle with snipped cilantro or oregano if desired.

Home-style Scrambled Eggs

4 eggs
3 tablespoons water
¾ teaspoon salt
¼ cup margarine or butter
1 cup cubed cooked potato (1 medium)
3 tablespoons finely chopped onion
1 small zucchini, halved and sliced
1 tomato, chopped

Beat eggs, water and salt with fork. Heat margarine in 10-inch skillet over medium heat until melted; cook and stir vegetables in margarine 2 minutes. Pour egg mixture into skillet.

As mixture begins to set at bottom and side, gently lift cooked portions with spatula so that thin, uncooked portion can flow to bottom. Avoid constant stirring. Cook until eggs are thickened throughout but still moist, 3 to 5 minutes.

TO MICROWAVE: Omit margarine. Beat eggs, water and salt with fork in 1½-quart microwavable casserole. Stir in potato, onion and zucchini. Cover tightly and microwave on high (100%), stirring every minute, until eggs are puffy and set but still moist, 4 to 5 minutes. (Eggs will continue to cook while standing.) Stir in tomato.

Following pages: Home-style Scrambled Eggs (left) and Crabmeat Frittata

EGGS AND CHEESE

Baked Apple and Cheese Pancake

4 SERVINGS

¼ cup margarine or butter
1 cup all-purpose flour
1 cup milk
½ teaspoon salt
4 eggs
1 cup shredded Swiss, white Cheddar or
    Monterey Jack cheese (4 ounces)
½ lemon
2 medium apples or pears, thinly sliced
Powdered sugar

Heat oven to 425°. Heat margarine in rectangular pan, 13 x 9 x 2 inches, in oven until hot and bubbly. Beat flour, milk, salt and eggs until well blended. Pour into pan.

Bake until sides of pancake are puffed and deep golden brown, 20 to 25 minutes. Sprinkle with cheese. Squeeze juice from lemon over apples; arrange in center of pancake. Sprinkle with powdered sugar.

Broccoli Welsh Rabbit

3 SERVINGS

1 package (10 ounces) frozen broccoli spears
1 can (11 ounces) condensed Cheddar cheese
    soup
½ teaspoon dry mustard
½ teaspoon Worcestershire sauce
3 slices toast, cut into triangles
Coarsely ground pepper

Cook broccoli as directed on package; drain. Heat soup, mustard and Worcestershire sauce over medium heat, stirring frequently, until hot.

Arrange toast triangles on 3 dinner plates. Top each with 1 or 2 broccoli spears. Spoon cheese sauce over broccoli and toast; sprinkle with pepper.

Asparagus Welsh Rabbit: Substitute 1 package (10 ounces) frozen asparagus spears for the broccoli.

Baked Apple and Cheese Pancake

Pasta

One of the great things about pasta is that it is available in as many shapes as there are sauces. We've matched particular types and sauces in this chapter, but feel free to experiment. Don't forget the pepper mill and a generous bowl of freshly grated Parmesan cheese on the side.

Pasta Shells with Chicken and Broccoli

6 SERVINGS

1 cup chopped broccoli
1/3 cup chopped onion
2 cloves garlic, finely chopped
1 carrot, cut into very thin strips
3 tablespoons vegetable oil
2 cups cut-up cooked chicken or turkey
1 teaspoon salt
2 medium tomatoes, chopped
4 cups hot cooked shell or cartwheel macaroni
1/3 cup grated Parmesan cheese
2 tablespoons snipped parsley

Cook and stir broccoli, onion, garlic and carrot in oil in 10-inch skillet over medium heat until broccoli is crisp-tender, about 10 minutes.

Stir in chicken, salt and tomatoes; heat just until chicken is hot, about 3 minutes. Spoon over macaroni. Sprinkle with cheese and parsley.

Pasta Shells with Chicken and Broccoli

Chinese Noodles with Chicken and Vegetables

4 SERVINGS

4 boneless skinless chicken breast halves (about
   1½ pounds)
2 tablespoons vegetable oil
1 tablespoon finely chopped gingerroot
3 cloves garlic, finely chopped
1 package (14 ounces) chopped vegetables for
   stir-fry or chop suey (about 5 cups)
1 can (4 ounces) mushroom stems and pieces,
   undrained
1 tablespoon instant chicken bouillon
½ cup cold water
1 tablespoon cornstarch
1 tablespoon soy sauce
5 ounces uncooked Chinese noodles
1 teaspoon sesame oil

Cut chicken into ¼-inch slices. Heat vegetable oil in 12-inch skillet or wok until hot. Cook and stir chicken, gingerroot and garlic in oil over medium-high heat until chicken is white, 3 to 4 minutes.

Stir in vegetables, mushrooms and bouillon (dry); cook and stir until vegetables are crisp-tender, about 5 minutes. Mix cold water, cornstarch and soy sauce; stir into chicken mixture. Heat to boiling, stirring constantly. Boil and stir 1 minute.

Cook noodles as directed on package; drain. Toss with sesame oil. Add noodles to chicken mixture in skillet; toss until well coated. Serve with additional soy sauce if desired.

Linguine with Chicken and Artichokes

4 SERVINGS

6 ounces uncooked linguine or spaghetti
1 jar (6 ounces) marinated artichoke hearts
2 tablespoons olive or vegetable oil
1 medium onion, coarsely chopped
2 cups cut-up cooked chicken or turkey
1 cup frozen green peas
⅛ pound sliced fully cooked smoked ham, cut
   into ¼-inch strips (½ cup)*
1 tablespoon snipped fresh oregano leaves or 1
   teaspoon dried oregano leaves
¼ teaspoon pepper
1 container (8 ounces) dairy sour cream

Cook linguine as directed on package; drain.

Drain liquid from artichoke hearts into 10-inch skillet; cut artichoke hearts into halves and reserve. Add oil to artichoke liquid. Cook and stir onion in oil mixture until tender.

Stir artichoke hearts, chicken, peas, ham, oregano and pepper into onion mixture; cook and stir until hot. Remove from heat; stir in sour cream. Toss hot linguine with sauce.

✱ 6 slices bacon, crisply cooked and crumbled, can be substituted for the ham.

Cartwheel Pasta Primavera

2 cups uncooked cartwheel or shell macaroni
(about 8 ounces)

4 ounces mushrooms, sliced

10 stalks asparagus or 1 medium zucchini, cut
into bite-size pieces, or 1 cup frozen green
peas, thawed

2 tablespoons margarine or butter

1 3/4 cups milk

1/2 package (2.8-ounce size) creamy herb recipe
soup mix (1 envelope)

8 cherry tomatoes, cut into halves

1 package (2.5 ounces) smoked sliced ham, cut
up

1/4 cup grated Parmesan cheese

Cook macaroni as directed on package; drain. Cook and stir mushrooms and asparagus in margarine in 2-quart saucepan over medium heat until tender.

Mix milk and soup mix (dry) thoroughly; stir into mushroom mixture. Heat to boiling, stirring frequently; reduce heat. Stir in tomatoes and ham; heat until hot. Toss hot macaroni with sauce; sprinkle with cheese.

Following pages: Linguine with Chicken and Artichokes (left) and Cartwheel Pasta Primavera

Vermicelli with Smoked Fish and Gruyère

4 SERVINGS

8 ounces uncooked vermicelli
1 package (10 ounces) frozen chopped spinach
1 cup shredded Gruyère or Swiss cheese (4 ounces)
1/4 cup half-and-half
2 tablespoons margarine or butter
1/2 pound smoked whitefish, skinned, boned and flaked into 1-inch pieces (about 2 cups)

Cook vermicelli as directed on package except add frozen spinach to water before heating water to boiling; drain.

Toss with cheese, half-and-half and margarine. Turn onto hot platter; arrange fish on top.

Spaghetti with White Clam Sauce

4 SERVINGS

1 package (6 or 7 ounces) uncooked spaghetti
1/4 cup margarine or butter
2 cloves garlic, finely chopped
2 tablespoons snipped parsley
2 cans (6 1/2 ounces each) minced clams, undrained
1/2 cup grated Parmesan cheese
Snipped parsley

Cook spaghetti as directed on package; drain. Heat margarine in saucepan until melted; cook and stir garlic in margarine until light brown. Stir in 2 tablespoons parsley and the clams.

Heat to boiling; reduce heat. Simmer uncovered 3 to 5 minutes to blend flavors. Pour over hot spaghetti; toss. Sprinkle with cheese and parsley.

Mostaccioli with Prosciutto and Pine Nuts

8 ounces uncooked mostaccioli (about 3 cups)
1 bunch green onions (with tops), sliced
¼ cup pine nuts, pistachio nuts or slivered
  almonds
½ teaspoon seasoned salt
⅓ cup margarine or butter
¼ pound prosciutto or thinly sliced fully cooked
  smoked ham, cut into thin strips
1 cup freshly grated Parmesan cheese

Cook mostaccioli as directed on package; drain. Cook and stir onions, pine nuts and seasoned salt in margarine in 10-inch skillet over medium heat until onions are tender, about 3 minutes.

Toss onion mixture, prosciutto, ½ cup of the cheese and the hot mostaccioli. Sprinkle with remaining cheese.

Double Cheese Tortellini

2 cans (16 ounces each) stewed tomatoes
½ teaspoon dried oregano leaves
1 package (7.05 ounces) uncooked dried cheese-
  filled tortellini
1 cup shredded Cheddar cheese (4 ounces)

Heat tomatoes and oregano to boiling in 3-quart saucepan; stir in tortellini. Heat to boiling; reduce heat.

Boil gently, stirring occasionally, until tortellini is of desired doneness, 20 to 25 minutes. (Add 1 to 2 tablespoons water during last 5 minutes of cooking, if necessary, to prevent sticking.) Top each serving with ¼ cup cheese.

Cincinnati-style Chili

1 pound ground beef
3 medium onions, chopped
1 tablespoon chili powder
1 teaspoon salt
1 can (16 ounces) whole tomatoes, undrained
1 can (15½ ounces) kidney beans, undrained
1 can (8 ounces) tomato sauce
1 package (6 or 7 ounces) uncooked spaghetti
1¼ cups shredded Cheddar cheese (5 ounces)

Cook and stir ground beef and about 1 cup of the onions in 3-quart saucepan until beef is brown and onions are tender; drain. Stir in chili powder, salt, tomatoes, beans and tomato sauce; break up tomatoes. Cook uncovered over medium heat until of desired consistency, about 10 minutes.

Cook spaghetti as directed on package; drain. For each serving, spoon about ¾ cup beef mixture over 1 cup hot spaghetti. Sprinkle each serving with ¼ cup cheese and about 2 tablespoons remaining onion.

Top with dollop of dairy sour cream and sliced hot chili if desired.

TO MICROWAVE: Crumble ground beef into 2-quart microwavable casserole; add 1 cup of the onions. Cover loosely and microwave on high (100%) 3 minutes; break up beef and stir. Cover loosely and microwave until very little pink remains in beef, 2 to 5 minutes longer; drain.

Stir in tomatoes; break up. Stir in chili powder, salt, beans and tomato sauce. Cover tightly and microwave 8 minutes; stir. Cover tightly and microwave until hot and bubbly, 6 to 9 minutes longer. Continue as directed above.

Cincinnati-style Chili

Macaroni and Cheese with Green Chilies

6 SERVINGS

3 cups uncooked shell macaroni (about 12 ounces)

½ cup shredded Cheddar cheese (2 ounces)

½ cup sliced ripe olives

1 cup half-and-half

½ teaspoon salt

½ cup chopped mild green chilies or 1 can (4 ounces) chopped green chilies, drained

½ cup chopped red bell pepper or 1 jar (2 ounces) diced pimientos, drained

Cook macaroni as directed on package; drain. Stir in remaining ingredients. Cook over low heat, stirring occasionally, until cheese is melted and sauce is hot, about 5 minutes.

Macaroni and Cheese with Tomato

4 SERVINGS

4 slices bacon, cut into 1-inch pieces

1 medium onion, chopped

1 medium green pepper, chopped

1 package (7 ounces) uncooked elbow macaroni (2 cups)

1 can (10¾ ounces) condensed tomato soup

1½ soup cans water

2 cups shredded American or colby cheese (8 ounces)

Cook bacon in 10-inch skillet, stirring frequently, until crisp. Stir in onion and green pepper; cook and stir until vegetables are tender. Stir in macaroni, soup and water.

Heat to boiling, stirring once or twice; reduce heat. Cover and simmer, stirring occasionally, until macaroni is tender, about 20 minutes. Stir in cheese until melted. Top each serving with buttered bread or cracker crumbs if desired.

TO MICROWAVE: Substitute 1¾ cups hot water for the 1½ soup cans water. Place bacon in 3-quart microwavable casserole. Cover loosely and microwave on high (100%) until crisp, 4 to 5 minutes.

Stir in onion, green pepper, macaroni, soup and hot water. Cover tightly and microwave 8 minutes; stir. Cover tightly and microwave, stirring every 4 minutes, until macaroni is tender, 6 to 8 minutes longer. Stir in cheese until melted.

Macaroni and Cheese with Green Chilies

Vermicelli with Lemony Green Vegetables

1 package (7 ounces) uncooked vermicelli
4 cups mixed bite-size pieces green vegetables
    (asparagus, broccoli, Chinese pea pods, green
    beans, zucchini)
1/4 cup margarine or butter
1 tablespoon grated lemon peel
1/2 cup milk
1 package (3 ounces) cream cheese, cut into
    cubes and softened
1/2 cup grated Parmesan cheese
Salt and pepper to taste

Cook vermicelli as directed on package; drain. Cook vegetables in margarine in 10-inch skillet over medium heat, stirring frequently, until crisp-tender, about 7 minutes; toss with lemon peel. Remove vegetables; keep warm.

Heat milk and cream cheese in skillet until smooth and creamy; stir in Parmesan cheese, salt and pepper. Toss with hot vermicelli. Serve vegetables over vermicelli and, if desired, with lemon wedges and coarsely ground pepper.

Herbed Tricolor Pasta

8 ounces uncooked vegetable-flavored rotini
    (about 3 cups)
2 teaspooons snipped fresh savory leaves or 1/2
    teaspoon dried savory leaves, crushed
1/4 cup whipping cream
6 ounces herb-flavored Havarti cheese, shredded
2 small summer squash, thinly sliced
Coarsely ground pepper

Cook rotini as directed on package except add savory to water; drain.

Stir in whipping cream, cheese and squash until cheese is melted. Arrange on platter; sprinkle with pepper. Garnish with fresh savory leaves if desired.

Vermicelli with Lemony Green Vegetables

Skillet Dishes

Of course this is the largest chapter in SmartCook. *Isn't your trusty skillet the most-used pan in the kitchen? An attractive ceramic skillet can even double as a serving dish. For a change of pace, try pasta, brown rice or couscous (which cooks in 5 minutes!) instead of regular white rice as an accompaniment.*

Chicken Livers with Glazed Apples

5 SERVINGS

1 pound chicken livers, each cut into halves or fourths
3 green onions (with tops), sliced
2 tablespoons margarine or butter
½ teaspoon salt
2 medium pared or unpared cooking apples, each cut into eighths
¼ cup packed brown sugar

Cook chicken livers and onions in margarine in 10-inch skillet over medium heat, stirring occasionally, until livers are brown, about 6 minutes. Sprinkle with salt. Move to one side of skillet.

Arrange apples in skillet; sprinkle with brown sugar. Cook uncovered over medium heat, stirring occasionally, until apples are tender and glazed, about 8 minutes. Serve apples and sauce over livers. Garnish with green onion tops if desired.

Chicken Livers with Glazed Apples (top) and Dilled Lemon Chicken

Dilled Lemon Chicken

6 small boneless skinless chicken breast halves
  (about 1½ pounds)
¼ cup margarine or butter
½ cup dry white wine
1 tablespoon lemon juice
¼ teaspoon salt
⅛ teaspoon dried dill weed
½ lemon, thinly sliced
2 green onions (with tops), sliced

Cook chicken breast halves in margarine in 10-inch skillet, turning once, until light brown, about 5 minutes on each side. Mix wine, lemon juice, salt and dill weed; pour over chicken. Place lemon slices on chicken.

Heat to boiling; reduce heat. Cover and simmer until chicken is done, 10 to 15 minutes. Remove chicken; keep warm. Heat wine mixture to boiling; cook until reduced to about half, about 3 minutes. Pour over chicken; sprinkle with onions.

TO MICROWAVE: Prepare chicken breast halves as directed above. Decrease margarine to 2 tablespoons and wine to ¼ cup. Place margarine in 3-quart microwavable casserole. Microwave uncovered on high (100%) until melted, about 1½ minutes. Arrange chicken, with thickest pieces to outside edge, in margarine. Cover tightly and microwave 4 minutes.

Mix wine, lemon juice, salt and dill weed; pour over chicken. Place lemon slices on chicken; rotate casserole ½ turn. Cover tightly and microwave until chicken is done, 4 to 6 minutes longer. Let stand covered 5 minutes; sprinkle with onions.

Chicken with Tomatoes and Leeks

3 slices bacon
4 small boneless skinless chicken breast halves
    (about 1 pound)
2 medium leeks, cut lengthwise into halves and
    sliced
2 tablespoons margarine or butter
1 can (5 ounces) evaporated milk
2 teaspoons snipped fresh tarragon leaves or 1/2
    teaspoon dried tarragon leaves
1/4 teaspoon red pepper sauce
4 Italian plum tomatoes or 2 medium tomatoes,
    chopped
Salt and pepper to taste

Cook bacon in 10-inch skillet until crisp; drain, reserving fat in skillet. Cook chicken breast halves in fat over medium heat, turning once, until done, 12 to 14 minutes. Remove chicken from skillet; cover and reserve. Drain fat from skillet.

Cook and stir leeks in margarine in skillet until crisp-tender, 5 to 7 minutes. Stir in milk, tarragon and red pepper sauce. Heat to boiling, stirring occasionally. Boil and stir until slightly thickened.

Crumble bacon; stir bacon, chicken and tomatoes into skillet. Heat over medium heat, spooning sauce over chicken, until chicken is hot, about 2 minutes. Sprinkle with salt and pepper.

Easy Chicken Curry

2 tablespoons margarine or butter
1 teaspoon curry powder
1 small onion, chopped
2 cups cut-up cooked chicken or turkey
1/3 cup raisins
1 small unpared all-purpose red apple, coarsely
    chopped
1 can (10¾ ounces) condensed cream of chicken
    soup
1 soup can water
Hot cooked rice
Chopped peanuts

Cook and stir margarine, curry powder and onion in 3-quart saucepan over medium heat until onion is tender, about 4 minutes.

Stir in remaining ingredients except rice and peanuts. Cook, stirring occasionally, until hot. Serve over rice; sprinkle with peanuts and, if desired, additional raisins.

NOTE: Stir hot cooked green peas into rice before serving if desired.

Following pages: Chicken with Tomatoes and Leeks (left) and Easy Chicken Curry

Chicken with White Wine Sauce

4 boneless skinless chicken breast halves (about
   1½ pounds)
1 tablespoon vegetable oil
½ cup whipping cream
¼ cup dry white wine
1 teaspoon Dijon-style mustard
½ teaspoon salt
6 green onions (with tops), cut into 1-inch pieces

Cut each chicken breast half lengthwise into 3 pieces. Cook chicken in oil in 10-inch skillet over medium heat, turning occasionally, until white. Stir in remaining ingredients.

Heat to boiling over medium-high heat. Continue boiling, stirring occasionally, until sauce is slightly thickened, about 15 minutes. Garnish with green onion tops, cut into thin slices.

Orange-glazed Chicken and Carrots

1 package (6¾ ounces) instant long grain and
   wild rice
1 tablespoon vegetable oil
2 large boneless skinless chicken breast halves
   (about ¾ pound), cut into 1½-inch pieces
1 package (16 ounces) frozen whole baby carrots
1 can (6 ounces) frozen orange juice
   concentrate, thawed
1 juice can water
2 tablespoons honey
2 tablespoons cornstarch
1 teaspoon dry mustard
2 tablespoons cold water

Prepare instant rice as directed on package; keep warm. Heat oil in 10-inch skillet over medium heat until hot. Cook and stir chicken in oil until white.

Stir in carrots, orange juice, juice can water and honey. Heat to boiling; reduce heat to medium. Cook uncovered, stirring occasionally, until carrots are done, 10 to 12 minutes.

Mix cornstarch and mustard; stir in cold water. Stir into chicken mixture. Heat to boiling, stirring constantly. Boil and stir 1 minute. Serve with rice.

Glazed Turkey Tenderloins

4 SERVINGS

2 turkey breast tenderloins (about 1 pound)
1 tablespoon vegetable oil
⅓ cup orange marmalade
1 teaspoon finely chopped gingerroot or ½
   teaspoon ground ginger
1 teaspoon Worcestershire sauce

Cook turkey breast tenderloins in oil in 10-inch skillet over medium heat until brown on one side, about 5 minutes; turn turkey. Stir in remaining ingredients; reduce heat.

Cover and simmer, stirring occasionally, until turkey is done and sauce is thickened, about 15 minutes. Cut turkey into thin slices; spoon sauce over turkey.

Oriental Turkey and Vegetables

4 SERVINGS

1 can (10¾ ounces) condensed chicken broth
3 tablespoons cornstarch
1 broth can water
1 teaspoon finely chopped gingerroot
2 cups cut-up cooked turkey or chicken
1 package (16 ounces) frozen Oriental-style
   vegetables
Chow mein noodles

Gradually stir broth into cornstarch in 3-quart saucepan until mixture is smooth. Stir in water and gingerroot. Cook over medium heat, stirring constantly, until mixture thickens and boils. Boil and stir 1 minute.

Stir in turkey and vegetables. Heat to boiling; reduce heat. Cover and cook, stirring occasionally, until vegetables are tender. Serve over chow mein noodles and, if desired, with soy sauce.

TO MICROWAVE: Place vegetables in 3-quart microwavable casserole. Cover tightly and microwave on high (100%) until almost tender, as directed in microwave directions on package. Stir in broth, gingerroot and turkey.

Decrease water to ½ cup cold water; mix cornstarch and water. Stir into vegetable mixture. Cover tightly and microwave 3 minutes; stir. Cover tightly and microwave, stirring every minute, until mixture thickens and boils, 5 to 6 minutes longer. Serve as directed above.

Italian-style Turkey Patties

1 pound ground turkey
¼ cup dry bread crumbs
1 tablespoon lemon juice
1 tablespoon olive oil
1 teaspoon salt
1 teaspoon rubbed sage
¼ teaspoon pepper
3 slices provolone cheese or about 6 tablespoons
    shredded mozzarella cheese
1 tablespoon margarine or butter
6 cups shredded cabbage
Salt and pepper to taste

Mix ground turkey, bread crumbs, lemon juice, oil, salt, sage and pepper. Shape mixture into 6 thin patties, each about 5 inches in diameter. Cut each slice cheese into halves. Place half-slice cheese on half of each patty; fold patty over cheese. Carefully press edge to seal.

Heat margarine in 12-inch skillet over medium heat until melted and bubbly. Cook patties in margarine until done, about 4 minutes on each side. Remove patties from skillet; keep warm.

Cook and stir cabbage in drippings in skillet until wilted, about 5 minutes. Sprinkle with salt and pepper. Serve with turkey patties; garnish with lemon wedges if desired.

Ingredients for Italian-style Turkey Patties

Sole with Red Grapes

1½ pounds sole fillets
1¼ cups water
⅓ cup dry white wine
1 tablespoon lemon juice
½ teaspoon salt
¼ teaspoon pepper
3 green onions (with tops), sliced
½ cup whipping cream
2 tablespoons all-purpose flour
1 cup seedless red or green grapes

If fish fillets are large, cut into 6 serving pieces. Place fish in 10-inch skillet; add water, wine, lemon juice, salt, pepper and onions. Heat to boiling; reduce heat. Cover and simmer until fish flakes easily with fork, 5 to 6 minutes. Remove fish with slotted spatula; keep warm.

Shake whipping cream and flour in tightly covered container; stir into liquid in skillet. Heat to boiling. Continue boiling, stirring frequently, until slightly thickened, about 10 minutes. Add grapes; heat until hot. Spoon sauce over fish.

TO MICROWAVE: Decrease water to ¾ cup and wine to ¼ cup. Arrange fish, with thickest parts to outside edges, in rectangular microwavable dish, 11 x 7 x 1½ inches. Sprinkle with lemon juice, salt, pepper and onions. Cover with vented plastic wrap and microwave on high (100%) 4 minutes; rotate dish ½ turn. Microwave until fish flakes easily with fork, 3 to 4 minutes longer. Let stand covered.

Place water and wine in 4-cup microwavable measure. Shake whipping cream and flour in tightly covered container; gradually stir into wine mixture. Microwave uncovered on high (100%) to boiling, 3 to 4 minutes, stirring every minute. Stir in grapes. Serve sauce over fish.

Fish Fillets with Green Peppers and Mushrooms

1 pound fish fillets
3 tablespoons soy sauce
¼ teaspoon ground ginger
1 clove garlic, finely chopped
2 medium green peppers, cut into 1-inch pieces
8 ounces mushrooms, cut into halves
3 tablespoons vegetable oil

If fish fillets are large, cut into 4 serving pieces. Mix soy sauce, ginger and garlic; brush on both sides of fish. Cook and stir green peppers and mushrooms in oil in 10-inch skillet over medium-high heat until crisp-tender, about 6 minutes. Remove vegetables with slotted spoon; reserve.

Cook fish in same skillet until fish flakes easily with fork, about 8 minutes. Add vegetables; heat just until hot. Serve with hot cooked rice or Oriental noodles if desired.

TO MICROWAVE: Omit oil. Cut fish fillets into 4 serving pieces. Mix soy sauce, ginger and garlic; brush on both sides of fish. Arrange fish, with thickest parts to outside edges, in square microwavable dish, 8 x 8 x 2 inches. Top with vegetables. Cover with vented plastic wrap and microwave on high (100%) 4 minutes; rotate dish ½ turn. Microwave until fish flakes easily with fork and vegetables are crisp-tender, 4 to 5 minutes longer.

Following pages: Sole with Red Grapes

Salmon Steaks with Asparagus and Peas

4 small salmon or halibut steaks, each about 1
  inch thick (about 1 1/2 pounds)
1/2 teaspoon salt
1/2 teaspoon dried rosemary leaves, crushed
1/4 cup water
1 tablespoon lemon juice
1/2 pound asparagus, cut into 2-inch pieces
1 cup fresh or frozen green peas
Lemon wedges

Arrange fish steaks in 10-inch skillet; sprinkle with salt and rosemary. Pour water and lemon juice into skillet. Heat to boiling; reduce heat. Cover and cook until fish is firm, about 8 minutes.

Arrange asparagus and peas on fish in skillet. Cover and simmer until vegetables are crisp-tender and fish flakes easily with fork, about 6 minutes. Remove fish and vegetables with slotted spoon. Serve with lemon wedges.

TO MICROWAVE: Omit water. Arrange fish steaks in square microwavable dish, 8 x 8 x 2 inches. Sprinkle with salt, rosemary and lemon juice. Arrange asparagus and peas on fish. Cover with vented plastic wrap and microwave on high (100%) 5 minutes; rotate dish 1/2 turn. Microwave until fish flakes easily with fork and vegetables are crisp-tender, 4 to 5 minutes longer. Serve with lemon wedges.

Salmon Steaks with Asparagus and Peas

Oriental Fish Fillets with Bok Choy

½ pound bok choy
1 tablespoon sesame seed
1 tablespoon vegetable oil
1 bunch green onions (with tops), cut into 2-inch
  pieces
1 small red pepper, cut into 1-inch pieces
1 pound fish fillets (cod, monkfish, orange
  roughy), cut into 1-inch pieces
½ cup chicken broth
½ teaspoon red pepper flakes
1 tablespoon cornstarch
1 tablespoon teriyaki sauce
Hot cooked rice

Remove leaves from bok choy; cut leaves into ½-inch strips. Cut stems into ¼-inch slices. Cook sesame seed in oil in 10-inch skillet over medium heat, stirring occasionally, until golden brown. Add bok choy stems, onions, red pepper, fish, broth and pepper flakes. Heat to boiling; reduce heat. Cover and simmer until fish is white, about 5 minutes.

Mix cornstarch and teriyaki sauce; gradually stir into skillet. Heat to boiling, stirring constantly. Boil and stir 1 minute. Stir in bok choy leaves until wilted. Serve over rice.

Fish Steaks on Steamed Vegetables

1 tablespoon margarine or butter
1 medium onion, sliced and separated into rings
1 small yellow pepper, cut into 1/4-inch slices
1 small red pepper, cut into 1/4-inch slices
8 ounces spinach, coarsely chopped (about 6 cups)
4 small fish steaks, each about 1 inch thick (about 1 1/2 pounds) *
1 tablespoon snipped fresh savory leaves or 1 teaspoon dried savory leaves
Salt and pepper to taste
4 thin slices lemon

Heat margarine in 10-inch skillet until melted. Layer onion, yellow and red peppers, spinach and fish steaks in skillet (skillet will be full). Sprinkle with savory, salt and pepper. Place lemon slice on each fish steak.

Cover and cook over low heat 15 minutes. Uncover and cook until fish flakes easily with fork and liquid is reduced, 15 to 20 minutes longer.

✱ 1 or 2 large fish steaks can be used; cut into 4 serving pieces.

TO MICROWAVE: Arrange fish steaks, with thickest parts to outside edges, in square microwavable dish, 8 x 8 x 2 inches. Sprinkle with savory, salt and pepper; place lemon slice on each fish steak. Cover with vented plastic wrap and microwave on high (100%) 4 minutes; rotate dish 1/2 turn. Microwave until fish flakes easily with fork, 4 to 5 minutes longer. Let stand covered.

Place margarine, onion and yellow and red peppers in 1 1/2-quart microwavable casserole. Cover tightly and microwave on high (100%) until vegetables are crisp-tender, 3 to 4 minutes; stir in spinach. Cover tightly and microwave just until spinach is hot, 1 to 2 minutes. Serve fish over vegetables.

Following pages: Ingredients for Fish Steaks on Steamed Vegetables

Stir-fried Scallops and Pea Pods

4 SERVINGS

1 pound scallops
1 tablespoon packed brown sugar
1 tablespoon soy sauce
2 teaspoons cornstarch
6 slices bacon, cut into 1-inch pieces
6 green onions (with tops), cut into 1-inch pieces
1 can (8 ounces) sliced water chestnuts, drained
4 ounces fresh Chinese pea pods or 1 package (6 ounces) frozen Chinese pea pods, thawed

If scallops are large, cut into halves. Toss scallops, brown sugar, soy sauce and cornstarch in bowl; cover and refrigerate 10 minutes.

Cook and stir bacon in 10-inch skillet or wok over medium heat until crisp. Drain, reserving 1 tablespoon fat in skillet; reserve bacon.

Cook and stir scallops, onions and water chestnuts in bacon fat over medium-high heat until scallops are white, about 7 minutes; stir in pea pods. Stir in bacon just before serving.

Scallops with Broccoli and Mushrooms

4 SERVINGS

1 pound scallops
4 ounces mushrooms, sliced (about 1 1/2 cups)
2 tablespoons margarine or butter
2 cups cut-up broccoli or 1 package (10 ounces) frozen chopped broccoli, thawed
1 jar (2 ounces) sliced pimientos, drained
1 can (10 3/4 ounces) condensed chicken broth
3 tablespoons cornstarch
2 teaspoons soy sauce
Hot cooked rice or pasta

If scallops are large, cut into halves. Cook and stir mushrooms in margarine in 3-quart saucepan over medium heat until tender, about 5 minutes. Stir in scallops, broccoli and pimientos. Cook, stirring frequently, until scallops are white, 3 to 4 minutes.

Gradually stir chicken broth into cornstarch until smooth. Stir broth mixture and soy sauce into scallop mixture. Heat to boiling, stirring constantly. Boil and stir 1 minute. Serve over rice.

Stir-fried Scallops and Pea Pods

Sautéed Beef Tenderloin

1-pound beef tenderloin, about 6 inches long
1 tablespoon margarine or butter
Salt and pepper to taste
1 medium onion, sliced and separated into rings
1 clove garlic, crushed
1/3 cup dry red wine
1 jar (4 1/2 ounces) whole mushrooms, drained

Cut beef tenderloin into 8 slices, each about ¾ inch thick. Heat margarine in 10-inch skillet until melted. Cook beef in margarine over medium heat, turning once, until brown and center is medium rare, 3 to 4 minutes on each side. Remove beef to warm platter; sprinkle with salt and pepper.

Add onion and garlic to skillet; cook and stir until onion is crisp-tender, 3 to 4 minutes. Stir in wine and mushrooms; cook and stir until hot. Pour onion mixture over beef.

Sweet-and-Sour Beef

1-pound beef flank steak
3 tablespoons vegetable oil
1 medium onion, cut into 1-inch pieces
1 can (8 ounces) pineapple chunks in juice,
   undrained
1/4 cup sugar
1/4 cup white vinegar
1 tablespoon instant chicken bouillon
1 tablespoon soy sauce
1 tablespoon cornstarch
1 tablespoon cold water
1 medium green pepper, cut into 1-inch pieces
2 medium tomatoes, each cut into eighths

Cut beef with grain into 2-inch strips. Cut strips across grain into 1/8-inch slices.

Heat oil in 12-inch skillet or wok over medium-high heat until hot. Add beef and onion; cook and stir until beef is brown, about 3 minutes. Stir in pineapple, sugar, vinegar, bouillon (dry) and soy sauce. Heat to boiling.

Mix cornstarch and cold water; stir into beef mixture. Cook and stir 1 minute. Stir in green pepper and tomatoes; cook and stir 1 minute. Serve with hot cooked rice if desired.

Raw ingredients for making Sautéed Beef Tenderloin

Stir-fried Orange Beef

1-pound beef boneless sirloin steak
3 tablespoons vegetable oil
¼ teaspoon ground ginger
¼ teaspoon garlic powder
2 tablespoons vegetable oil
3 cups fresh vegetable pieces*
1 cup orange juice
½ cup cold water
2 tablespoons cornstarch
2 tablespoons soy sauce
Hot cooked rice

Cut beef steak with grain into 2-inch strips. Cut strips across grain into ⅛-inch slices. Heat 12-inch skillet or wok until 1 or 2 drops of water bubble and skitter when sprinkled in skillet. Add 3 tablespoons oil; rotate skillet to coat side. Add beef and sprinkle with ginger and garlic powder; cook and stir until beef is brown, about 3 minutes. Remove beef from skillet.

Add 2 tablespoons oil to skillet; rotate skillet to coat side. Add vegetables; cook and stir 1 minute. Stir in beef and orange juice; heat to boiling. Mix cold water, cornstarch and soy sauce; stir into beef mixture. Cook and stir until thickened, about 1 minute. Serve with rice.

* For quick preparation, vegetables of your choice (such as sliced mushrooms, broccoli flowerets, cauliflowerets, sliced carrots, celery, onion or green pepper) can be purchased ready for cooking from a salad bar.

Hamburgers Parmigiana

1 pound ground beef
1 small onion, chopped
2 tablespoons grated Parmesan cheese
1/2 teaspoon garlic salt
1 jar (15 1/2 ounces) chunky-style spaghetti sauce
1/2 cup shredded mozzarella cheese
4 slices French bread, toasted, or 2 hamburger
    buns, split and toasted

Mix ground beef, onion, Parmesan cheese and garlic salt. Shape into 4 patties, each about 1/2 inch thick. Cook in 10-inch skillet over medium heat, turning frequently, until of desired doneness; drain.

Pour spaghetti sauce over patties; heat until hot. Top each patty with 2 tablespoons mozzarella cheese; let stand until cheese begins to melt. Serve on French bread.

Creamy Beef and Green Beans

1 pound ground beef
1 medium onion, chopped
2 tablespoons steak sauce
1/2 package (16-ounce size) frozen French-style
    green beans
1 can (10 3/4 ounces) condensed cream of celery
    soup
1 can (4 ounces) mushroom stems and pieces,
    undrained
1 cup garlic-flavored croutons

Cook and stir ground beef and onion in 10-inch skillet until beef is brown; drain. Stir in remaining ingredients except croutons.

Heat to boiling; reduce heat. Cover and simmer, stirring occasionally, until of desired consistency, about 10 minutes. Sprinkle with croutons.

Easy Tacos

1 pound ground beef
1 large onion, chopped
1 envelope (about 1¼ ounces) taco seasoning
   mix
1 cup water
1 package (12 ounces) tortilla chips
½ head lettuce, shredded
2 medium tomatoes, chopped
1 can (2¼ ounces) sliced ripe olives, drained
1 cup shredded Cheddar or Monterey Jack cheese
   (4 ounces)
⅔ cup dairy sour cream

Cook and stir ground beef and onion in 10-inch skillet until beef is brown; drain. Stir in seasoning mix (dry) and water.

Heat to boiling; reduce heat. Simmer uncovered 10 minutes, stirring occasionally. Spoon beef mixture onto chips. Top with remaining ingredients.

TO MICROWAVE: Crumble ground beef into 2-quart microwavable casserole; add onion. Cover loosely and microwave on high (100%) 3 minutes; break up beef and stir. Cover loosely and microwave until very little pink remains in beef, 2 to 5 minutes longer; drain.

Stir in seasoning mix (dry) and ¾ cup water. Microwave uncovered on high (100%) 3 minutes; stir. Microwave uncovered until hot, 2 to 5 minutes longer. Continue as directed above.

Barbecued Beef and Beans

1 pound ground beef
1 teaspoon chili powder
1 teaspoon garlic salt
1 can (16 ounces) barbecue beans
1 can (10¾ ounces) condensed tomato soup
1 can (4 ounces) chopped green chilies
1 cup shredded American or Monterey Jack
   cheese (4 ounces)

Mix ground beef, chili powder and garlic salt. Shape into 6 patties, each about ½ inch thick. Cook in 10-inch skillet over medium heat, turning frequently, until brown. Remove patties from skillet; drain drippings from skillet.

Stir beans, soup and chilies into skillet until well mixed; place patties on top. Heat to boiling; reduce heat. Cover and simmer until patties are of desired doneness, about 5 minutes.

Sprinkle with cheese; cover and let stand until cheese is melted, about 2 minutes. Serve over corn bread or toasted hamburger buns if desired.

Sloppy Joes with Potatoes and Onion

4 SERVINGS

1 pound lean ground beef
Salt and pepper to taste
1 medium onion, sliced and separated into rings
2 medium potatoes, thinly sliced
1 can (15½ ounces) Sloppy Joe sauce

Crumble ground beef into 10-inch skillet; sprinkle with salt and pepper. Layer onion and potatoes on beef; pour sauce over top.

Cover and cook over low heat until beef is done and potatoes are tender, about 30 minutes.

TO MICROWAVE: Crumble ground beef into 2-quart microwavable casserole; sprinkle with salt and pepper. Layer onion and potatoes on beef. Cover tightly and microwave on high (100%) 5 minutes; rotate casserole ½ turn. Microwave 5 minutes longer.

Stir 1 teaspoon sugar into sauce; pour sauce over potatoes. Cover tightly and microwave 5 minutes; rotate casserole ½ turn. Microwave until potatoes are tender, 5 to 6 minutes longer.

Veal Chops with Browned Onions

4 SERVINGS

1 tablespoon margarine or butter
1 tablespoon vegetable oil
4 veal rib chops, each about ¾ inch thick
½ package (16-ounce size) frozen small whole onions
2 small zucchini, cut into ½-inch pieces
Salt and pepper to taste

Heat margarine and oil in 10-inch skillet until margarine is melted. Arrange veal chops and onions in skillet. Cook uncovered over medium heat, turning onions often, until veal is brown, about 7 minutes.

Turn veal; add zucchini. Cover and cook until onions and zucchini are tender, about 5 minutes. Sprinkle with salt and pepper.

Veal Patties with Pears

1 pound ground veal
¼ cup butter cracker crumbs (about 6 round
  crackers)
¾ teaspoon ground allspice
½ teaspoon salt
¼ teaspoon pepper
1 egg
1 tablespoon margarine or butter
¼ cup slivered almonds
2 small firm unpared pears, cut into ½-inch
  slices
1 cup apple juice
2 teaspoons cornstarch

Mix ground veal, cracker crumbs, allspice, salt, pepper and egg. Shape into 4 patties, each about ¾ inch thick. Heat margarine in 10-inch skillet over medium heat until melted. Cook patties in margarine, turning once, until brown and no longer pink in center, 7 to 8 minutes on each side. Remove patties; keep warm.

Add almonds and pears to skillet. Mix apple juice and cornstarch until smooth; stir into skillet. Heat to boiling, stirring constantly. Boil and stir 1 minute. Pour sauce and pears over veal.

Turkey Patties with Pears: Substitute 1 pound ground turkey for the veal.

Veal Chow Mein

1 pound coarsely ground veal
2 medium stalks celery, sliced
1 medium onion, sliced
2 cups bean sprouts (about 4 ounces)
1 tablespoon soy sauce
1 can (10½ ounces) condensed beef broth
1 can (4 ounces) mushroom stems and pieces,
  undrained
¼ cup cold water
2 tablespoons cornstarch
Chow mein noodles

Cook and stir ground veal, celery and onion in 10-inch skillet over medium heat until veal is brown. Stir in bean sprouts, soy sauce, broth and mushrooms.

Heat to boiling, stirring occasionally. Mix cold water and cornstarch; gradually stir into veal mixture. Heat to boiling, stirring constantly. Boil and stir 1 minute. Serve over chow mein noodles.

Lamb Patties with Summer Squash (top) and Veal Patties with Pears

Lamb Patties with Summer Squash

4 SERVINGS

1 pound ground lamb
½ teaspoon garlic salt
¼ teaspoon pepper
2 small onions, cut into fourths
1 small green pepper, sliced
1 small summer squash, cut into ½-inch slices
1 tablespoon snipped fresh marjoram leaves or 1
    teaspoon dried marjoram leaves

Mix lamb, garlic salt and pepper. Shape into 4 patties, each about ½ inch thick. Cook patties in 10-inch skillet over medium heat until light brown, about 5 minutes; turn.

Arrange vegetables around patties; sprinkle with marjoram. Cover and cook until lamb is done and vegetables are crisp-tender, about 8 minutes.

TO MICROWAVE: Prepare patties as directed above. Arrange on microwavable rack. Cover with waxed paper and microwave on high (100%) 4 minutes.

Arrange vegetables on and around lamb; sprinkle with marjoram. Cover with waxed paper and microwave 4 minutes; rotate rack ½ turn. Microwave until vegetables are crisp-tender and lamb is done, 3 to 5 minutes longer.

Greek-style Lamb and Orzo

4 SERVINGS

1 pound ground lamb or beef
1 can (16 ounces) stewed tomatoes
1 stalk celery, cut into ½-inch pieces
½ cup orzo
½ teaspoon salt
¼ teaspoon ground red pepper
Plain yogurt

Cook and stir ground lamb in 10-inch skillet until light brown; drain. Stir in remaining ingredients except yogurt. Heat to boiling; reduce heat.

Cover and simmer, stirring frequently, until tomato liquid is absorbed and orzo is tender, about 12 minutes. Serve with yogurt.

TO MICROWAVE: Crumble ground lamb into 2-quart microwavable casserole. Cover with waxed paper and microwave on high (100%) 3 minutes; stir. Cover with waxed paper and microwave until no longer pink, 2 to 3 minutes longer; drain.

Stir in remaining ingredients except yogurt. Cover tightly and microwave 4 minutes; stir. Cover tightly and microwave, stirring every 2 minutes, until orzo is tender, 8 to 10 minutes longer. Serve with yogurt.

Ground Lamb Stroganoff

1 pound ground lamb
1 medium onion, chopped
1 can (10¾ ounces) condensed cream of chicken
    soup
1 can (4 ounces) mushroom stems and pieces,
    drained
½ teaspoon seasoned salt
¼ teaspoon pepper
½ cup dairy sour cream or plain yogurt
Hot buttered spinach noodles
1 medium carrot, finely shredded

Cook and stir ground lamb and onion in 10-inch skillet until lamb is brown; drain. Stir in soup, mushrooms, seasoned salt and pepper. Heat to boiling; reduce heat. Simmer uncovered, stirring frequently, 5 minutes.

Stir in sour cream; heat just until hot. Serve over noodles; sprinkle with carrot.

Ground Beef Stroganoff: Substitute 1 pound ground beef for the lamb.

TO MICROWAVE: Crumble ground lamb into 2-quart microwavable casserole; add onion. Cover with waxed paper and microwave on high (100%) 3 minutes; stir. Cover with waxed paper and microwave until no longer pink, 2 to 3 minutes longer; drain.

Stir in soup, mushrooms, seasoned salt and pepper. Cover tightly and microwave 3 minutes; stir. Cover tightly and microwave to boiling, 2 to 3 minutes longer. Stir in sour cream. Cover tightly and microwave until hot, 1 to 2 minutes. Serve over noodles; sprinkle with carrot.

Pork Chops with Brussels Sprouts

4 SERVINGS

4 pork loin or rib chops, each about ½ inch thick
2 tablespoons margarine or butter
½ package (24-ounce size) frozen home-style
    potato wedges
1 green or red pepper, chopped
½ package (16-ounce size) frozen Brussels
    sprouts*
½ cup dry white wine or apple juice
½ cup water
1½ teaspoons snipped fresh basil leaves or ½
    teaspoon dried basil leaves
1 teaspoon garlic salt
¼ teaspoon pepper
2 teaspoons cornstarch
2 teaspoons water

Cook pork chops in margarine in 10-inch skillet over medium heat until brown on both sides. Remove pork; keep warm. Cook potatoes and green pepper in skillet, stirring occasionally, until potatoes are light brown, about 6 minutes.

Return pork to skillet; place Brussels sprouts on pork. Add wine, ½ cup water, the basil, garlic salt and pepper. Heat to boiling; reduce heat. Cover and simmer until pork is done and vegetables are tender, about 15 minutes. Remove pork; keep warm.

Mix cornstarch and 2 teaspoons water; stir into vegetables in skillet. Heat to boiling, stirring constantly. Boil and stir 1 minute. Serve vegetables with pork.

✱ ½ pound fresh Brussels sprouts can be substituted for the frozen Brussels sprouts.

Pork Tenderloin with Apples

6 SERVINGS

1½ pounds pork tenderloin
1 tablespoon margarine or butter
1 tablespoon vegetable oil
Salt and pepper to taste
8 ounces mushrooms, sliced
2 unpared cooking apples, cut into cubes
½ cup whipping cream
¼ cup apple cider or chicken broth
1 tablespoon Dijon-style mustard

Cut pork tenderloin diagonally into ¼-inch slices. Cook a few slices pork at a time in margarine and oil in 10-inch skillet over medium heat until light brown on both sides. Sprinkle with salt and pepper. Remove pork; keep warm.

Cook mushrooms and apples in skillet, stirring occasionally, until tender and liquid is evaporated. Stir in remaining ingredients. Heat to boiling, stirring constantly. Pour over pork. Sprinkle with snipped parsley if desired.

Pork Chop with Brussels Sprouts

Gingered Pork with Nectarines

1 pound pork boneless shoulder or loin
1 tablespoon dry white wine
1 tablespoon soy sauce
1 teaspoon cornstarch
1 teaspoon sugar
3 tablespoons vegetable oil
1 teaspoon finely chopped gingerroot or
    1 teaspoon ground ginger
1 green pepper, cut into 1-inch pieces
1 can (8 ounces) sliced water chestnuts, drained
¼ cup cold water
2 tablespoons cornstarch
1 cup chicken broth
2 large nectarines, sliced*
½ cup salted nuts
Cooked Chinese noodles or rice

Cut pork with grain into 2-inch strips. Cut strips across grain into ⅛-inch slices. Toss pork, wine, soy sauce, 1 teaspoon cornstarch and the sugar in glass or plastic bowl. Cover and refrigerate 20 minutes.

Heat 12-inch skillet or wok until 1 or 2 drops of water bubble and skitter when sprinkled in skillet. Add oil; rotate skillet to coat bottom. Add pork and gingerroot; cook and stir until pork is no longer pink. Add green pepper and water chestnuts; cook and stir 1 minute.

Mix cold water and 2 tablespoons cornstarch; stir broth and cornstarch mixture into pork mixture. Heat to boiling. Boil and stir 1 minute; stir in nectarines. Sprinkle with nuts. Serve with noodles.

✳ 1 can (16 ounces) sliced peaches, drained, can be substituted for the nectarines.

TO MICROWAVE: Omit oil and decrease broth to ¾ cup. Toss pork, wine, soy sauce, 1 teaspoon cornstarch, the sugar and gingerroot in 2-quart microwavable casserole. Cover tightly and refrigerate 20 minutes. Microwave tightly covered on high (100%) 4 minutes; stir. Cover tightly and microwave until no longer pink, 3 to 4 minutes longer.

Stir in green pepper, water chestnuts and broth. Mix cold water and 2 tablespoons cornstarch; stir into pork mixture. Cover tightly and microwave 2 minutes; stir. Cover tightly and microwave to boiling, 4 to 5 minutes, stirring every minute; stir in nectarines. Sprinkle with nuts. Serve with noodles.

Gingered Pork with Nectarines

Szechuan-style Pork

1 pound pork boneless loin or leg
1 tablespoon soy sauce
2 teaspoons cornstarch
½ teaspoon ground red pepper
1 clove garlic, finely chopped
2 tablespoons vegetable oil
3 cups broccoli flowerets or 1 package (16 ounces) frozen broccoli cuts, thawed
2 small onions, cut into eighths
1 can (8 ounces) whole water chestnuts, drained
¼ cup chicken broth
½ cup peanuts
Hot cooked rice

Cut pork into slices, 2 x 1 x ⅛ inch. Toss pork, soy sauce, cornstarch, red pepper and garlic in glass or plastic bowl. Cover and refrigerate 20 minutes.

Heat 12-inch skillet or wok until 1 or 2 drops of water bubble and skitter when sprinkled in skillet. Add oil; rotate skillet to coat bottom. Add pork; cook and stir until no longer pink. Add broccoli, onions and water chestnuts; cook and stir 2 minutes. Stir in broth; heat to boiling. Stir in peanuts. Serve with rice.

TO MICROWAVE: Increase cornstarch to 1 tablespoon. Omit oil. Cut pork as directed above. Toss pork, soy sauce, cornstarch, red pepper and garlic in 3-quart microwavable casserole. Cover tightly and refrigerate 20 minutes. Microwave tightly covered on high (100%) 4 minutes; stir. Cover tightly and microwave until no longer pink, 5 to 6 minutes longer.

Stir in broccoli, onions, water chestnuts and broth. Cover tightly and microwave 3 minutes; stir. Cover tightly and microwave until broccoli is crisp-tender, 3 to 4 minutes longer. Stir in peanuts. Serve with rice.

Ham and Hominy

1 small onion, chopped
½ small green pepper, chopped
2 tablespoons margarine or butter
¼ cup milk
1 package (3 ounces) cream cheese, cut into cubes
2 cups cut-up fully cooked smoked ham
1 can (20 ounces) hominy, drained
1 cup shredded spinach

Cook and stir onion and green pepper in margarine in 3-quart saucepan over medium heat until onion is tender, about 5 minutes.

Stir in milk and cream cheese. Cook, stirring constantly, until cheese is melted. Stir in ham and hominy; heat, stirring occasionally, until hot. Remove from heat; stir in spinach until wilted.

TO MICROWAVE: Place onion, green pepper and margarine in 2-quart microwavable casserole. Cover with waxed paper and microwave on high (100%) 2 minutes; stir. Cover with waxed paper and microwave until onion is tender, 1 to 2 minutes longer.

Stir in milk and cream cheese. Microwave uncovered, stirring every minute, until cheese is melted, 3 to 4 minutes. Stir in ham and hominy. Cover tightly and microwave, stirring every 2 minutes, until hot, 4 to 6 minutes. Stir in spinach until wilted.

Ham and Zucchini with Poppy Seed

1 medium onion, thinly sliced
2 tablespoons margarine or butter
3 cups cut-up fully cooked smoked ham
4 small zucchini (about 1 pound), cut into ¼-inch strips
1 green pepper, cut into ¼-inch slices
⅛ teaspoon pepper
½ cup dairy sour cream
1 teaspoon poppy seed

Cook and stir onion in margarine in 10-inch skillet until tender. Stir in ham, zucchini, green pepper and pepper. Cover and cook over medium heat, stirring occasionally, until vegetables are crisp-tender, about 8 minutes.

Stir in sour cream and poppy seed; heat just until hot. Serve with hot cooked rice or noodles if desired.

Braised Knackwurst Dinner

2 cups water
2 teaspoons instant beef bouillon
2 large potatoes, cut lengthwise into fourths
4 medium carrots, cut into 3 x ½-inch strips
2 large onions, cut into fourths
½ medium head cabbage, cut into 4 wedges
1 teaspoon salt
1 medium apple, cut into wedges
4 to 6 knackwurst
Prepared mustard
Prepared horseradish

Heat water and bouillon (dry) to boiling in 4-quart Dutch oven. Layer potatoes, carrots, onions and cabbage in bouillon; sprinkle with salt. Layer apple and knackwurst on top. Heat to boiling; reduce heat. Cover and simmer until vegetables are tender, 25 to 30 minutes.

Remove knackwurst, apple and vegetables with slotted spoon. Serve with mustard and horseradish.

Bratwurst and Sauerkraut

1 tablespoon margarine or butter
1 pound fully cooked bratwurst
2 cans (16 ounces each) sauerkraut, drained
⅓ cup packed brown sugar

Heat margarine in 10-inch skillet until melted. Cook bratwurst in margarine over medium heat, turning frequently, until brown, about 5 minutes. Add sauerkraut; sprinkle with brown sugar. Cover and cook over low heat until hot, about 10 minutes.

TO MICROWAVE: Omit margarine. Arrange bratwurst in ungreased square microwavable dish, 8 x 8 x 2 inches. Add sauerkraut; sprinkle with brown sugar. Cover with vented plastic wrap and microwave on high (100%), rotating dish ½ turn every 5 minutes, until hot, 10 to 12 minutes.

Braised Knackwurst Dinner

Grilled or Broiled Dishes

For sheer succulence, it's hard to beat a juicy steak cooked to smoky perfection over glowing coals. Top it with a pat of nutty Sesame Butter for the easiest of suppers. When the weather's less than accommodating, the broiler or microwave can often take over—with equally delicious results.

Grilled Italian Sausage Kabobs

6 SERVINGS

¹/₂ cup pizza sauce
1 tablespoon dried basil leaves
1 tablespoon vegetable oil
1¹/₂ pounds Italian-style sausage links, cut into 1¹/₂-inch pieces
2 medium zucchini, cut into 1-inch pieces
1 medium red pepper, cut into 1¹/₂-inch pieces
1 medium green pepper, cut into 1¹/₂-inch pieces
6 large pimiento-stuffed olives

Mix pizza sauce, basil and oil; reserve. Cook sausage pieces over medium heat until partially cooked, about 10 minutes; drain. Alternate sausage pieces, zucchini pieces and pepper pieces on each of 6 metal skewers, leaving space between foods. Place olive on tip of each skewer.

Cover and grill kabobs 5 to 6 inches from medium coals, turning and brushing 2 or 3 times with pizza sauce mixture, until sausage is done and vegetables are crisp-tender, 20 to 25 minutes.

TO BROIL: Set oven control to broil. Broil sausage pieces until partially cooked; prepare sauce and kabobs as directed above. Place kabobs on rack in broiler pan. Broil with tops about 5 inches from heat, turning and brushing 2 or 3 times with pizza sauce mixture, until sausage is done and vegetables are tender, about 15 minutes.

Grilled Italian Sausage Kabobs

Country Broiled Chicken

6 SERVINGS

2½-pound broiler-fryer chicken, cut up
½ cup margarine or butter
¼ cup vegetable oil
2 tablespoons lemon juice
2 teaspoons salt
2 teaspoons sugar
½ teaspoon paprika
½ teaspoon ground ginger
1 small onion, finely chopped
1 clove garlic, crushed

Place chicken pieces, skin sides down, on rack in broiler pan. Heat remaining ingredients, stirring occasionally, until margarine is melted; brush over chicken.

Set oven control to broil. Broil chicken with tops 5 to 7 inches from heat, brushing with margarine mixture every 10 to 15 minutes and turning chicken as it browns, until thickest pieces are done, 40 to 50 minutes.

Herbed Cube Steak in Foil

1 SERVING

1 beef cubed steak
½ cup whole kernel corn
1 slice tomato, ¼ inch thick
1 slice onion
2 to 3 small fresh mushrooms
2 tablespoons margarine or butter
1 to 2 teaspoons snipped fresh herb leaves if desired
Salt and pepper to taste

Place beef cubed steak on heavy-duty aluminum foil. Place corn, tomato and onion to each side; place mushrooms on top. Top steak and mushrooms with margarine. Sprinkle with herbs, salt and pepper.

Wrap securely in foil. Place packet on cooking grill or on coals. Cook, turning once, until done, 35 to 40 minutes on grill, 15 to 20 minutes on coals.

Monterey Fish Steaks

1½ pounds swordfish, halibut or salmon steaks,
    each ¾ to 1 inch thick
1 teaspoon salt
¼ teaspoon pepper
¼ cup margarine or butter, melted
1 tablespoon snipped fresh chervil leaves or
    1 teaspoon dried chervil leaves
1 tablespoon lemon juice
Avocado Sauce or Caper Sauce (below)
Lemon wedges

Sprinkle fish steaks with salt and pepper. Mix margarine, chervil and lemon juice.

Cover and grill fish about 4 inches from medium coals, turning once and brushing 2 or 3 times with margarine mixture, until fish flakes easily with fork, 15 to 25 minutes. Cut into serving pieces. Serve with sauce and lemon wedges.

AVOCADO SAUCE

1 small avocado, peeled and cut up
⅓ cup dairy sour cream
1 teaspoon lemon juice
¼ teaspoon salt
Few drops red pepper sauce

Beat all ingredients with hand beater until smooth.

CAPER SAUCE

1 lemon
¼ cup capers, drained
1 tablespoon snipped parsley
1 tablespoon margarine or butter
¼ teaspoon salt

Pare and section lemon; remove seeds. Chop lemon; mix with remaining ingredients. Heat until hot.

TO MICROWAVE: Sprinkle fish steaks with salt and pepper. Arrange fish, with thickest parts to outside edges, in square microwavable dish, 8 x 8 x 2 inches.

Mix margarine, chervil and lemon juice; drizzle over fish. Cover tightly and microwave on high (100%) 4 minutes; rotate dish ½ turn. Microwave until fish flakes easily with fork, 4 to 7 minutes longer. Let stand covered 3 minutes. Cut into serving pieces. Serve as directed above.

GRILLED OR BROILED DISHES

Fish Fillets with Flavored Butters

1½ pounds fish fillets, each ½ to ¾ inch thick
Flavored Butters (below)

Cover and grill fish fillets about 4 inches from medium coals, turning and brushing occasionally with one of the flavored butters, until fish flakes easily with fork, 15 to 25 minutes. Cut into serving pieces; top with a flavored butter.

TO MICROWAVE: Cut fish fillets into serving pieces. Place margarine for one of the flavored butters in square microwavable dish, 8 x 8 x 2 inches. Cover tightly and microwave on high (100%) until melted, 30 to 60 seconds. Stir in remaining ingredients for flavored butter.

Arrange fish, with thickest parts to outside edges, in dish; turn fish to coat well. Cover tightly and microwave 4 minutes; turn fish over and rearrange in dish. Cover tightly and microwave until fish flakes easily with fork, 3 to 5 minutes longer. Let stand covered 3 minutes.

GARLIC BUTTER

2 tablespoons margarine or butter, softened
1 teaspoon snipped fresh oregano leaves or
   ½ teaspoon dried oregano leaves
½ teaspoon paprika
1 clove garlic, crushed
Dash of freshly ground pepper

Mix all ingredients.

LEMON BUTTER

2 tablespoons margarine or butter, melted
½ teaspoon grated lemon peel
1 tablespoon lemon juice
½ teaspoon Worcestershire sauce

Mix all ingredients.

PEPPERY MUSTARD BUTTER

2 tablespoons margarine or butter, softened
1½ teaspoons dry mustard
½ teaspoon lemon pepper

Mix all ingredients.

Broiled Fish Steaks

3 fish steaks, each about 1 inch thick (about
 1 pound)
½ teaspoon salt
Dash of pepper
2 tablespoons margarine or butter, melted

Sprinkle both sides of fish steaks with salt and pepper; brush with half of the margarine.

Set oven control to broil. Place fish on rack in broiler pan. Broil with tops about 4 inches from heat until light brown, about 6 minutes; brush fish with margarine. Turn carefully; brush with margarine. Broil until fish flakes very easily with fork and is opaque in center, 4 to 6 minutes longer.

TO BROIL FISH FILLETS: Substitute 1 pound fish fillets for the steaks. For fish fillets less than ¾ inch thick, brush with all of the margarine. Continue as directed above except broil with tops about 4 inches from heat until fish flakes very easily with fork and is opaque in center, 5 to 6 minutes (do not turn).

Following pages: Fish Fillet with Lemon Butter (left) and Broiled Steak with Sesame Butter

Broiled Steak with Flavored Butters

1/3- to 3/4-pound steak with bone or 1/3- to
  1/2-pound boneless steak per serving
Salt and pepper to taste
Flavored Butters (below)

Choose beef tenderloin (filet mignon), T-bone, porterhouse, sirloin, rib or rib eye steak. Slash outer edge of fat on steak diagonally at 1-inch intervals to prevent curling (do not cut into lean).

Set oven control to broil. Place steak on rack in broiler pan; place broiler pan so top of 3/4- to 1-inch steak is 2 to 3 inches from heat, 1- to 2-inch steak is 3 to 5 inches from heat. Broil, turning once, until desired doneness (see Timetable).

Sprinkle with salt and pepper after turning and after removing from broiler; top with flavored butter.

TO GRILL: Grill steak 4 to 5 inches from medium coals, turning once, until desired doneness (see Timetable). Serve as directed above.

HERB BUTTER

1/4 cup margarine or butter, softened
1 to 2 tablespoons snipped fresh herb leaves
  (basil, chives, oregano, savory, tarragon or
  thyme)
1 teaspoon lemon juice
1/4 teaspoon salt

Beat all ingredients.

MUSTARD BUTTER

1/4 cup margarine or butter, softened
1 tablespoon snipped parsley
2 tablespoons prepared mustard
1/4 teaspoon onion salt

Beat all ingredients.

SESAME BUTTER

¼ cup margarine or butter, softened
1 teaspoon Worcestershire sauce
½ teaspoon garlic salt
1 tablespoon toasted sesame seed

Beat margarine, Worcestershire sauce and garlic salt. Stir in sesame seed.

Timetable for Broiling or Grilling Beef Steak

CUT	APPROXIMATE TOTAL COOKING TIME*
Tenderloin (filet mignon, 4 to 8 ounces)	15 to 20 minutes
T-bone Steak	
1 inch	25 minutes
1½ inches	35 minutes
Porterhouse Steak	
1 inch	25 minutes
1½ inches	35 minutes
Sirloin Steak	
1 inch	25 minutes
1½ inches	35 minutes
Rib or Rib Eye Steak	
1 inch	20 minutes
1½ inches	30 minutes
2 inches	45 minutes

* Time given is for medium doneness (160°).

Following pages: Broiled Lamb Chops with Red Currant Sauce (left) and Garlic Mint Sauce

Grilled Lamb Chops

1 to 2 loin, rib or shoulder lamb chops per serving

Remove fell (the paperlike covering) if it is on chops. Slash outer edge of fat on lamb chops diagonally at 1-inch intervals to prevent curling (do not cut into lean).

Cover and grill lamb 5 to 6 inches from medium coals, turning and brushing 2 or 3 times with one of the sauces (below), until done (see Timetable). Serve with any remaining sauce.

TO BROIL: Prepare lamb chops as directed above. Set oven control to broil. Place lamb on rack in broiler pan; place broiler pan so tops of ¾- to 1-inch chops are 2 to 3 inches from heat, 1- to 2-inch chops are 3 to 5 inches from heat. Broil until brown. The chops should be about half done (see Timetable).

Sprinkle brown side with salt and pepper if desired. (Always season after browing because salt tends to draw moisture to surface, delaying browning.) Turn chops; broil until brown.

GARLIC MINT SAUCE

½ cup mint-flavored apple jelly
2 tablespoons water
2 cloves garlic, crushed

Heat all ingredients over medium heat, stirring constantly, until jelly is melted.

HERBED RED WINE SAUCE

¼ cup dry red wine
¼ cup chili sauce
¼ teaspoon dried oregano leaves, crushed
¼ teaspoon dried thyme leaves, crushed
¼ teaspoon dried rosemary leaves, crushed

Mix all ingredients.

ORANGE-GINGER SAUCE

¼ cup frozen orange juice concentrate, thawed
¼ cup soy sauce
1 teaspoon crushed gingerroot

Mix all ingredients.

RED CURRANT SAUCE

½ cup red currant jelly
1 tablespoon prepared mustard
1 tablespoon soy sauce

Heat all ingredients over medium heat, stirring constantly, until jelly is melted.

Timetable for Broiling or Grilling Lamb Chops

THICKNESS	APPROXIMATE TOTAL COOKING TIME*
¾ to 1 inch	12 minutes
1½ inches	18 minutes
2 inches	22 minutes

*Time given is for medium doneness (160°); lamb chops are not usually served rare.

Broiled Pork Chops and Onions

4 SERVINGS

4 pork loin or rib chops, each about ¾ inch thick
2 medium onions
Salt to taste
Rubbed sage to taste
2 teaspoons margarine or butter, melted
Pepper to taste

Set oven control to broil. Place pork chops on rack in broiler pan. Broil with tops 3 to 5 inches from heat until light brown, about 10 minutes. Turn pork.

Cut ¼-inch slice from both ends of each onion. Cut onions crosswise into halves; place in broiler pan with pork. Sprinkle salt and sage over onions. Broil until onions are light brown, about 5 minutes; turn onions. Sprinkle with salt and sage; drizzle with margarine. Broil until pork is done, about 5 minutes longer. Sprinkle salt and pepper over pork.

TO GRILL: Grill pork and onions 4 inches from medium coals, turning 1 or 2 times and brushing onions with margarine, until pork is done (170°), about 20 minutes. Sprinkle salt and sage over onions; sprinkle salt and pepper over pork.

Broiled Hamburgers

4 SERVINGS

1 pound ground beef
3 tablespoons finely chopped onion, if desired
3 tablespoons water
½ teaspoon salt
¼ teaspoon pepper

Mix all ingredients. Shape mixture into 4 patties, each about ¾ inch thick.

Set oven control to broil. Place patties on rack in broiler pan. Broil with tops about 3 inches from heat, turning once, until desired doneness, 5 to 7 minutes on each side for medium. About 1 minute before hamburgers are done, top each with cheese slice if desired. Broil until cheese is melted. Serve on toasted buns if desired.

TO GRILL: Prepare patties as directed above. Grill patties about 4 inches from medium coals, turning once, until desired doneness, 7 to 8 minutes on each side for medium. Brush barbecue sauce on patties before and after turning if desired. Serve on toasted buns if desired.

Broiled Pork Chops and Onions

Grilled Teriyaki Burgers

1 pound ground beef
2 tablespoons soy sauce
1 teaspoon salt
¼ teaspoon crushed gingerroot or ⅛ teaspoon
   ground ginger
1 clove garlic, crushed

Shape ground beef into 4 patties, each about ¾ inch thick. Mix remaining ingredients; spoon onto patties. Turn patties; let stand 10 minutes.

Grill patties about 4 inches from medium coals, turning once, until desired doneness, 5 to 7 minutes on each side for medium. Serve on toasted sesame seed buns if desired.

TO BROIL: Prepare patties as directed above. Set oven control to broil. Place patties on rack in broiler pan. Broil with tops about 3 inches from heat, turning once, until desired doneness, about 5 minutes on each side for medium. Serve on toasted sesame seed buns if desired.

Grilled Coney Island Burgers

6 SANDWICHES

1 pound ground beef
1 can (7½ ounces) chili with beans
1 tablespoon chopped green chilies
6 frankfurter buns, split and warmed

Shape ground beef into 6 rolls, each about 5 inches long and ¾ inch thick. Mix chili and green chilies in small grill pan; heat on grill until hot.

Grill ground beef rolls about 4 inches from medium coals, turning once, until desired doneness, 3 to 5 minutes on each side for medium. Serve in frankfurter buns; spoon about 2 tablespoons chili mixture into each bun.

TO BROIL: Mix chili and green chilies in saucepan; heat until hot. Prepare ground beef rolls as directed above. Set oven control to broil. Place rolls on rack in broiler pan. Broil with tops about 3 inches from heat, turning once, until desired doneness, about 3 minutes on each side for medium. Serve as directed above.

Grilled Teriyaki Burger

Broiled Deviled Burgers

1 pound ground beef
1 can (4½ ounces) deviled ham
1 small onion, finely chopped
¼ teaspoon salt
⅛ teaspoon garlic salt
⅛ teaspoon pepper
1 can (8 ounces) sauerkraut, drained
5 slices Swiss cheese, 3 x 3 inches

Mix all ingredients except sauerkraut and cheese. Shape mixture into 5 patties, each about ¾ inch thick.

Set oven control to broil. Place patties on rack in broiler pan. Broil with tops about 4 inches from heat, turning once, until desired doneness, 5 to 7 minutes on each side for medium. Top each patty with sauerkraut and cheese slice. Broil until cheese is light brown. Serve on toasted rye or pumpernickel buns if desired.

TO GRILL: Prepare patties as directed above. Grill patties about 4 inches from medium coals 3 minutes; turn patties and top each with sauerkraut and cheese slice. Grill until desired doneness, 2 to 4 minutes longer for medium.

TO MICROWAVE: Prepare patties as directed above. Arrange patties on microwavable rack in microwavable dish. Cover with waxed paper and microwave on high (100%) 3 minutes; rotate dish ½ turn. Microwave until patties are almost done, 2 to 4 minutes longer. Pour off drippings.

Top each patty with sauerkraut and cheese slice. Microwave uncovered 1 minute; rotate dish ½ turn. Microwave until cheese begins to melt, 30 to 90 seconds longer. Serve on toasted rye or pumpernickel buns if desired.

Broiled Burgers with Mushrooms and Onions

1 pound ground beef
3 tablespoons finely chopped onion
3 tablespoons water
¾ teaspoon salt
⅛ teaspoon pepper
Mushrooms and Onions (below)

Mix ground beef, onion, water, salt and pepper. Shape mixture into 4 patties, each about ¾ inch thick.

Set oven control to broil. Place patties on rack in broiler pan. Broil with tops about 3 inches from heat until desired doneness, 5 to 7 minutes on each side for medium. Prepare Mushrooms and Onions; spoon over hamburgers.

MUSHROOMS AND ONIONS

1 medium onion, thinly sliced
1 tablespoon margarine or butter
1 can (4 ounces) mushroom stems and pieces, drained
½ teaspoon Worcestershire sauce

Cook onion in margarine over medium heat, stirring occasionally, until tender. Stir in mushrooms and Worcestershire sauce; heat until mushrooms are hot.

TO GRILL: Prepare patties as directed above. Grill as directed for Grilled Hamburgers (page 125). Serve as directed above.

TO MICROWAVE: Prepare patties as directed above. Place patties on microwavable rack in microwavable dish. Cover with waxed paper and microwave on high (100%) 3 minutes; rotate dish ½ turn. Microwave until almost done, about 2 minutes longer. Let stand covered 3 minutes.

Place onion and margarine in 1-quart microwavable casserole. Cover tightly and microwave on high (100%) until onion is crisp-tender, about 2 minutes. Stir in mushrooms and Worcestershire sauce. Cover tightly and microwave until mushrooms are hot, about 1 minute. Spoon over hamburgers.

Sandwiches

There's something elemental about a well-stuffed sandwich—maybe because it's the ultimate in finger food. Since they're built around deli and bakery items and prepared condiments, the only cooking these combinations may require is a trip under the broiler.

Chicken and Artichoke Croissants

4 SANDWICHES

4 croissants, split lengthwise into halves
1 cup sliced mushrooms (about 3 ounces)
3 tablespoons margarine or butter
1 tablespoon all-purpose flour
½ teaspoon garlic salt
½ cup milk
¼ cup dry white wine
1 cup cut-up cooked chicken or turkey
½ cup shredded Swiss cheese (2 ounces)
1 jar (6 ounces) marinated artichoke hearts, drained and cut into halves

Heat croissants in 300° oven until hot, about 10 minutes. Cook and stir mushrooms in 2 tablespoons of the margarine in 1½-quart saucepan over medium heat until tender, 2 to 3 minutes. Remove mushrooms; reserve.

Heat remaining 1 tablespoon margarine in same saucepan until melted; stir in flour and garlic salt. Cook, stirring constantly, until bubbly. Remove from heat; stir in milk and wine. Heat to boiling, stirring constantly. Boil and stir 1 minute.

Stir in mushrooms and remaining ingredients; heat until hot. Spoon over croissant bottoms; add tops.

Chicken and Artichoke Croissant

131

Open-face Chicken Sandwiches

4 SANDWICHES

1½ cups cut-up cooked chicken or turkey
⅓ cup mayonnaise or salad dressing
¼ cup toasted slivered almonds
1 stalk celery, thinly sliced
1 green onion (with top), thinly sliced
1 medium tomato, sliced
2 whole wheat English muffins, split and toasted
1 container (6 ounces) frozen avocado dip, thawed

Mix chicken, mayonnaise, almonds, celery and onion. Arrange tomato slices on muffin halves. Spoon chicken mixture onto tomato. Spoon avocado dip onto chicken mixture.

Deli Sandwiches

8 SANDWICHES

Prepared mustard
8 frankfurter buns, split
1 pound thinly sliced cooked turkey or chicken
2 large dill pickles, cut lengthwise into fourths
½ pound thinly sliced fully cooked smoked ham
½ pound sliced Thuringer or salami
1 pint deli coleslaw (creamy style)

Spread mustard over cut sides of buns. Layer turkey, pickles, ham and Thuringer on bottom half of each bun; spoon about ¼ cup coleslaw onto each. Top with remaining bun half.

Broiled Seafood Sandwiches

1 cup mixed bite-size pieces cooked crabmeat,
    lobster or shrimp*
1 cup shredded Swiss cheese (4 ounces)
½ cup mayonnaise or salad dressing
1 green onion (with top), thinly sliced
4 slices whole grain bread, toasted
Alfalfa sprouts

Mix all ingredients except toast and sprouts. Set oven control to broil. Arrange sprouts on toast; top with seafood mixture.

Place sandwiches on ungreased cookie sheet. Broil with tops about 4 inches from heat until seafood mixture is hot and bubbly, about 2 minutes.

* 1 cup bite-size pieces cooked fish (salmon, cod, halibut, tuna, swordfish) can be substituted for the crabmeat, lobster or shrimp.

Shrimp and Avocado Club Sandwiches

Mayonnaise or salad dressing
12 slices white bread, toasted
4 lettuce leaves
12 slices tomatoes (about 2 medium)
12 slices bacon, crisply cooked
2 cans (4½ ounces each) large shrimp, rinsed
    and drained
1 large avocado, peeled and thinly sliced

Spread mayonnaise over one side of each slice toast. Place lettuce leaf, 3 slices tomato and 3 slices bacon on each of 4 slices toast. Top with another slice toast.

Arrange shrimp on top; arrange avocado slices on shrimp. Top with third slice toast; secure with wooden picks. Cut sandwiches diagonally into 4 triangles.

Turkey and Avocado Club Sandwiches: Substitute 4 slices cooked turkey or chicken for the shrimp.

Tunawiches

½ loaf (1-pound size) French bread
Spicy brown mustard
½ cup mayonnaise or salad dressing
2 cans (6½ ounces each) tuna, drained
1 cup shredded Muenster cheese (4 ounces)
Salad greens
1 medium cucumber, thinly sliced
1 medium tomato, cut into 6 slices

Cut loaf of bread lengthwise into halves; spread mustard over cut sides. Mix mayonnaise and tuna; spread on mustard.

Top with cheese, salad greens, cucumber and tomato. Cut each bread half into thirds. Spoon dollop of mayonnaise onto each sandwich if desired.

Tuna Cobb Salad Sandwiches

4 SANDWICHES

1 can (6½ ounces) tuna, drained
4 to 6 slices bacon, crisply cooked and crumbled
2 hard-cooked eggs, chopped
1 avocado, peeled and cut into cubes
¼ to ⅓ cup blue cheese dressing
Shredded iceberg or romaine lettuce
2 medium tomatoes, thinly sliced
4 croissants, split

Mix tuna, bacon, eggs, avocado and dressing. Place lettuce and tomatoes on bottom halves of croissants. Spoon tuna mixture on tomatoes; top with remaining halves.

Club Waldorf Sandwich Loaf

1-pound loaf unsliced oval Vienna or sourdough
   bread
Lettuce leaves
1 small onion, thinly sliced
¼ pound thinly sliced fully cooked smoked ham
¼ pound thinly sliced cooked turkey or chicken
4 ounces sliced provolone cheese
¼ cup lemon yogurt
¼ teaspoon curry powder
1 medium apple, chopped
1 stalk celery, chopped

Cut bread into sixteen ½-inch slices, not cutting completely through to bottom of loaf. Line every other slice with lettuce, onion, ham, turkey and cheese.

Mix remaining ingredients; spoon onto cheese. To serve, cut loaf between unfilled slices into sandwiches.

Beef Waldorf Sandwich Loaf: Substitute ½ pound thinly sliced roast beef for the ham and turkey. Substitute ¼ teaspoon dried dill weed for the curry powder.

Following pages: Hot Antipasto Poor Boys (left) and Spicy Lamb in Pita Breads

Hot Antipasto Poor Boys

4 OPEN-FACE SANDWICHES

¼ cup creamy Italian dressing
2 tablespoons grated Parmesan cheese
1 cup cherry tomatoes, cut into fourths
1 can (14 ounces) artichoke hearts, drained and
  cut into fourths
1 package (5 ounces) sliced pepperoni, cut up
1 can (2¼ ounces) sliced ripe olives, drained
2 poor boy buns, split*
½ cup shredded mozzarella cheese (2 ounces)

Mix dressing and Parmesan cheese in large bowl; toss with tomatoes, artichoke hearts, pepperoni and olives. Set oven control to broil. Place buns, cut sides up, on ungreased cookie sheet. Broil with tops about 6 inches from heat until golden brown, about 5 minutes.

Spoon pepperoni mixture onto buns. Sprinkle about 2 tablespoons mozzarella cheese over each. Broil until cheese is hot and bubbly, 3 to 4 minutes.

✱ 4 frankfurter buns, split, can be substituted for the poor boy buns. Sprinkle 1 tablespoon mozzarella cheese over pepperoni mixture on each bun. 8 open-face sandwiches (2 sandwiches per serving).

Spicy Lamb in Pita Breads

4 SANDWICHES

Yogurt Dressing (below)
1 pound ground lamb
1 small onion, chopped
1 clove garlic, crushed
1 tablespoon vegetable oil
½ teaspoon salt
½ teaspoon ground cumin
¼ teaspoon pepper
4 whole wheat pita breads (6-inch diameter)
Shredded lettuce
1 medium tomato, chopped

Prepare Yogurt Dressing. Cook and stir ground lamb, onion and garlic in oil over medium heat until lamb is brown; drain. Stir in salt, cumin and pepper.

Split each pita bread halfway around edge with knife; separate to form pocket. Spoon ¼ of the lamb mixture into each pocket. Top with lettuce and tomato. Serve with Yogurt Dressing.

YOGURT DRESSING

½ cup plain yogurt
1 tablespoon snipped fresh mint leaves or
  1 teaspoon dried mint leaves
1 teaspoon sugar
¼ small cucumber, seeded and chopped

Mix all ingredients; cover and refrigerate.

Sloppy Joes

1 pound ground beef
1 medium onion, chopped
1/3 cup chopped celery
1/3 cup chopped green pepper
1/3 cup catsup
1/4 cup water
1 tablespoon Worcestershire sauce
1/2 teaspoon salt
1/8 teaspoon red pepper sauce
6 hamburger buns, split and toasted

Cook and stir ground beef and onion in 10-inch skillet until beef is brown; drain. Stir in remaining ingredients except buns.

Cover and cook over low heat just until vegetables are tender, 10 to 15 minutes. Fill buns with beef mixture.

Chili Sloppy Joes: Stir in 1 can (4 ounces) chopped green chilies, drained, and 1 teaspoon chili powder with the celery.

TO MICROWAVE: Crumble ground beef into 2-quart microwavable casserole; add onion, celery and green pepper. Cover loosely and microwave on high (100%) 4 minutes; break up beef and stir. Cover loosely and microwave until very little pink remains in beef, 2 to 4 minutes longer; drain. Stir in remaining ingredients except buns. Cover tightly and microwave until hot, 3 to 5 minutes; stir. Fill buns with beef mixture.

Barbecued Roast Beef Sandwiches

Zesty Barbecue Sauce (below)
1 pound thinly sliced cooked roast beef, cut into
    1-inch strips (about 3 cups)
6 hamburger buns, split

ZESTY BARBECUE SAUCE

½ cup catsup
¼ cup vinegar
2 tablespoons chopped onion
1 tablespoon Worcestershire sauce
2 teaspoons packed brown sugar
¼ teaspoon dry mustard
1 clove garlic, crushed

Prepare Zesty Barbecue Sauce. Stir beef into sauce. Cover and simmer until beef is heated through, about 5 minutes. Fill each hamburger bun with beef mixture.

Heat all ingredients to boiling in 1-quart saucepan over medium heat, stirring constantly; reduce heat. Simmer uncovered 15 minutes, stirring sauce occasionally.

Quick Barbecued Roast Beef Sandwiches: Substitute 1 cup barbecue sauce for the Zesty Barbecue Sauce and 3 packages (3 ounces each) smoked sliced chicken, ham, turkey, beef or pastrami, cut into 1-inch strips, for the beef.

TO MICROWAVE: Mix sauce ingredients in 4-cup microwavable measure. Microwave uncovered on high (100%) 2 minutes; stir. Microwave uncovered until sauce is slightly thickened, 2 to 4 minutes longer. Stir beef into sauce. Cover tightly and microwave until beef is hot, 5 to 7 minutes.

Open-face Reubens

Prepared mustard
7 slices dark rye bread, toasted
1 can (8 ounces) sauerkraut, drained
1 package (3 ounces) sliced corned beef, finely snipped
2 cups shredded pizza or Swiss cheese (8 ounces)
¼ cup mayonnaise or salad dressing

Heat oven to 375°. Spread mustard lightly over one side of each slice toast; place mustard sides up on ungreased cookie sheet. Cut through sauerkraut with scissors. Stir in corned beef, cheese and mayonnaise.

Spread about ⅓ cup sauerkraut mixture on each slice toast. Bake until mixture is hot and cheese is melted, about 10 minutes. Cut sandwiches into halves if desired.

TO MICROWAVE: Spread mustard lightly over one side of each slice toast; arrange mustard sides up in circle on 10-inch microwavable plate lined with microwavable paper towels. Continue preparing sandwiches as directed above.

Microwave uncovered on high (100%) 2 minutes; rotate plate ½ turn. Microwave uncovered until cheese is melted and sauerkraut mixture is hot, 2 to 3½ minutes longer. Cut sandwiches into halves if desired.

Curried Egg and Shrimp Sandwiches

6 OPEN-FACE SANDWICHES

1 package (8 ounces) cream cheese, softened
1/4 cup dairy sour cream
1 teaspoon curry powder
1/4 teaspoon salt
6 slices multigrain bread, toasted
3 hard-cooked eggs, sliced
1 can (4 1/4 ounces) tiny shrimp, drained
1/4 cup finely chopped green onions (with tops)

Mix cream cheese, sour cream, curry powder and salt; spread over toast. Arrange egg slices on cream cheese mixture. Top with shrimp and onions.

Swiss Cheese and Vegetables in Pita Breads

6 SANDWICHES

1 cup shredded Swiss cheese (4 ounces)
1/2 cup thinly sliced cauliflowerets
1/4 cup mayonnaise or salad dressing
1 teaspoon snipped fresh dill weed or 1/2 teaspoon
   dried dill weed
1/2 teaspoon salt
1 medium tomato, chopped
1 small zucchini or carrot, shredded
3 pita breads (6-inch diameter), cut into halves
Salad greens

Mix all ingredients except pita breads and salad greens. Separate pita breads along cut sides to form pockets. Arrange salad greens and vegetable mixture in pockets.

Brie and Cucumber on Rye

½ English cucumber or 1 small cucumber
8 ounces Brie cheese, cut into ¼-inch pieces
¼ cup finely chopped green onions (with tops)
¼ cup oil-and-vinegar dressing
¾ teaspoon snipped fresh dill weed or
  ¼ teaspoon dried dill weed
Margarine or butter
4 slices rye bread
Salad greens

Cut cucumber lengthwise into halves; cut each half into thin slices. Toss cucumber, cheese, onions, dressing and dill weed.

Spread margarine over one side of each slice bread; top with salad greens. Spoon cheese mixture onto greens. Garnish each sandwich with 1 cooked shrimp and fresh dill weed if desired.

Zucchini and Cream Cheese on Rye: Substitute 1 medium zucchini for the English cucumber and 1 package (8 ounces) cream cheese for the Brie cheese.

Mozzarella and Tomato Melts

4 slices Italian bread, each 1 inch thick
8 ounces mozzarella cheese, sliced
2 medium tomatoes, thinly sliced
Salt and freshly ground pepper to taste
½ cup Pesto (below) or prepared pesto

Set oven control to broil. Place bread on ungreased cookie sheet. Broil with tops about 4 inches from heat until golden brown; turn. Divide cheese among bread slices. Broil just until cheese begins to melt.

Arrange tomatoes on cheese; sprinkle with salt and pepper. Top with Pesto. Garnish with fresh basil leaves if desired.

PESTO

2 cups firmly packed snipped fresh basil leaves
¾ cup grated Parmesan cheese
¾ cup olive oil
2 tablespoons pine nuts
4 cloves garlic

Place all ingredients in blender. Cover and blend on medium speed, stopping blender occasionally to scrape sides, until smooth, about 3 minutes.

NOTE: Freeze any remaining Pesto up to 6 months. Let stand at room temperature until thawed, at least 4 hours.

Grilled Peanut Butter and Banana

4 SANDWICHES

Peanut butter
8 slices English muffin bread
2 medium bananas
Margarine or butter, softened

Spread peanut butter over one side of 4 slices bread; slice bananas and arrange on top. Top with remaining bread; spread top slices with margarine.

Place sandwiches, margarine sides down, in skillet. Spread top slices with margarine. Cook uncovered over medium heat until bottoms are golden brown, about 4 minutes; turn. Cook until bottoms are golden brown and peanut butter is melted, 2 to 3 minutes longer.

Grilled Peanut Butter and Banana with Bacon: Place cooked bacon slices on bananas before topping with remaining bread.

Peanut Butter and Apples on Raisin Bread

4 SANDWICHES

¾ cup chunky peanut butter
¼ cup apricot preserves
1 teaspoon dry mustard
8 slices raisin bread
2 medium pared or unpared eating apples,
    thinly sliced
Salad greens

Mix peanut butter, preserves and mustard; spread over one side of 4 slices bread. Arrange apple slices and salad greens on peanut butter mixture. Top with remaining bread.

Desserts

For a quick finale, luscious seasonal fruit is the best place to start. While raspberries may not always be available, melon is a year-round staple. Add a dollop of yogurt, a splash of champagne, a scoop of ice cream or a drizzle of tangy fruit puree and you'll have a beautiful ending to any meal.

Honey Bee Sundaes

4 SERVINGS

½ cup honey
¼ cup apricot brandy
Chocolate chip, chocolate, coffee or vanilla ice cream
About 2 teaspoons uncooked ground coffee, powdered instant coffee or cocoa

Mix honey and brandy. Spoon over ice cream in each of 4 dessert dishes; sprinkle each with about ½ teaspoon coffee.

Honey Ambrosia

4 TO 6 SERVINGS

4 medium oranges, pared and thinly sliced
1 medium banana, sliced
½ cup orange juice
¼ cup honey
2 tablespoons lemon juice
¼ cup flaked coconut

Gently mix orange and banana slices. Mix orange juice, honey and lemon juice; pour over fruit. Sprinkle with coconut.

Honey Ambrosia (top) and Honey Bee Sundae

147

Watermelon with Blackberries and Pear Puree

6 SERVINGS

3 slices medium watermelon, each ¾ inch thick
1½ cups blackberries
Pear Puree (below)

Cut each watermelon slice into 10 wedges. Cut rind from wedges; remove seeds. Arrange wedges on 6 dessert plates; top with blackberries. Top each serving with Pear Puree.

PEAR PUREE

2 medium pears, pared
¼ cup light rum

Cut pears into fourths and remove cores and stems. Place pears and rum in workbowl of food processor fitted with steel blade or in blender container. Cover and process until smooth, about 1 minute.

Winter Fruit Compote

6 TO 8 SERVINGS

1 jar (17 ounces) figs, drained (reserve syrup)
1 jar (16 ounces) prunes, drained (reserve syrup)
3-inch cinnamon stick
1 can (29 ounces) peach halves, drained

Heat reserved syrups and the cinnamon stick to boiling in 2½-quart saucepan. Boil 5 minutes.

Add figs, prunes and peach halves; heat through. Remove cinnamon stick. Serve fruit warm in dessert dishes.

Orange Bavarian Cream

4 TO 6 SERVINGS

2 cartons (6 ounces each) orange yogurt
1 package (3½ ounces) vanilla instant pudding and pie filling
1 cup chilled whipping cream

Beat yogurt and pudding and pie filling (dry) in medium bowl on low speed 30 seconds. Beat in whipping cream on medium speed, scraping bowl occasionally, until soft peaks form, 3 to 5 minutes.

Layer in parfait glasses with fruit and crushed vanilla wafers, or serve over slices of angel food or pound cake. Garnish with mandarin orange segments if desired.

Oranges in Syrup

3 seedless oranges
1/2 cup water
1/3 cup sugar

Cut thin slivers of peel from 1 orange with vegetable parer or sharp knife, being careful not to cut into white membrane. Cover peel with boiling water. Let stand 5 minutes; drain.

Heat orange peel, water and sugar to boiling; reduce heat. Simmer uncovered until slightly thickened, 10 to 15 minutes; cool. Remove peel.

Pare oranges, cutting deep enough to remove all white membrane. Cut into slices. Pour syrup over slices; cover and refrigerate until chilled. Garnish with mint sprig if desired.

Starfruit and Strawberries in Champagne

6 SERVINGS

2 starfruit
1/4 cup sugar
2 cups strawberries, cut into halves
3/4 cup champagne or catawba juice

Cut starfruit crosswise into 1/4-inch slices. Sprinkle with sugar; let stand 30 minutes.

Spoon starfruit and strawberries into dessert dishes. Pour champagne over fruit.

Grapes and Blueberries with Yogurt

6 SERVINGS

2 cups seedless red grapes
1 cup blueberries
1/3 cup packed brown sugar
1 container (6 ounces) lemon yogurt
Ground nutmeg

Alternate layers of grapes, blueberries and brown sugar in 6 stemmed glasses. Top with yogurt; sprinkle with nutmeg.

Following pages: Starfruit and Strawberries with Champagne (left), Oranges in Syrup (center), and Grapes and Blueberries with Yogurt (right)

Baked Maple Apples

4 baking apples
4 teaspoons margarine or butter
4 tablespoons maple or maple-flavored syrup

Core baking apples (Rome Beauty, Golden Delicious, Greening). Pare 1-inch strip of skin from around middle of each apple, or pare upper half of each to prevent splitting.

Place apples upright in ungreased baking dish. Place 1 teaspoon margarine and 1 tablespoon syrup in center of each apple. Pour water (¼ inch deep) into baking dish.

Bake uncovered in 375° oven until tender when pierced with fork, 30 to 40 minutes. (Time will vary with size and variety of apples.) Spoon syrup in dish over apples several times during baking. Serve with cream if desired.

Melon with Sherbet and Berries

1 scoop sherbet or sorbet
1 melon slice or wedge
¼ cup berries

SUGGESTED COMBINATIONS

■ Cantataloupe or Persian melon; orange sherbet or sorbet; blackberries

■ Casaba melon; red raspberry or cranberry sherbet or sorbet; raspberries or strawberries

■ Crenshaw melon; lime sherbet or sorbet; blueberries or blackberries

■ Honeydew melon; lemon or pineapple sherbet or sorbet; blueberries, raspberries or strawberries

Baked Caramel Pears

4 TO 6 SERVINGS

4 firm pears, pared and cut into fourths
¼ cup packed brown sugar
2 tablespoons margarine or butter
½ cup whipping cream
4 to 6 tablespoons toasted coarsely
   chopped pecans

Heat oven to 400°. Arrange pears, round sides up, in single layer in ungreased square baking dish, 8 x 8 x 2 inches. Sprinkle with brown sugar; dot with margarine. Bake uncovered until sugar is bubbly and pears are tender, 35 to 40 minutes.

Pour whipping cream evenly over pears. Gently stir cream and syrup with fork until blended. Serve hot in heatproof dessert dishes. Sprinkle with pecans.

Baked Caramel Apples: Substitute 4 large tart cooking apples for the pears. Bake about 30 minutes.

Strawberries Romanoff

6 SERVINGS

1 quart strawberries, cut into halves
½ cup powdered sugar
3 to 4 tablespoons kirsch or orange-flavored
   liqueur
1 cup chilled whipping cream

Reserve 6 strawberry halves for garnish. Sprinkle remaining halves with powdered sugar and kirsch; toss. Cover and refrigerate 2 hours.

Just before serving, beat whipping cream in chilled medium bowl until soft peaks form; fold in strawberries. Garnish each serving with reserved strawberry half.

Pears Helene

1 cup sugar
2 cups water
1 teaspoon vanilla
3 medium pears, pared and cut into halves*
Hot Fudge Sauce (page 158)
Vanilla ice cream

Heat sugar and water to boiling in 10-inch skillet; reduce heat. Add vanilla. Place pears, cut sides down, in skillet; cover and simmer until tender, about 15 minutes. Turn pears over; refrigerate pears in syrup until chilled.

Just before serving, prepare Hot Fudge Sauce. Place 1 scoop ice cream in each of 6 dessert dishes. Top with pear half and 1 tablespoon Hot Fudge Sauce.

✱ 6 canned pear halves, drained, can be substituted for the sugar, water, vanilla and pears; refrigerate until chilled.

Summer Fruit Trifles

Vanilla Custard Sauce (page 159)
6 sponge cake cups
2 tablespoons cream sherry, if desired
3 cups cut-up fresh fruit
1/2 cup toasted sliced or slivered almonds

Prepare Vanilla Custard Sauce. Place each cake cup in dessert dish; drizzle with sherry. Top with fruit and custard sauce; sprinkle with almonds.

Almond-crusted Pound Cake

1 cup sliced almonds
1 package (16 ounces) golden pound cake mix
1/2 teaspoon almond extract

Heat oven to 325°. Generously grease loaf pan, 9 x 5 x 3 inches; sprinkle 1/2 cup almonds over bottom and 2/3 up sides, pressing if necessary.

Prepare cake mix as directed except add almond extract. Pour batter into pan. Sprinkle remaining almonds over batter. Bake as directed on package; cool 10 minutes. Remove from pan; cool.

Simple Fruit Desserts

- Serve fresh pineapple or peach slices in shallow dessert dishes topped with warm Amber Sauce (page 158).

- Pour ⅓ cup Vanilla Custard Sauce (page 159) onto dessert plate; tilt plate to cover bottom evenly. Spoon or pipe 2 to 3 tablespoons Raspberry Currant Sauce (page 159) onto custard sauce. Draw wooden pick through Raspberry Currant Sauce to make desired design. Top with raspberries.

- Serve fresh fruit topped with dollops of dairy sour cream or plain yogurt sweetened with brown sugar; sprinkle with additional brown sugar. Grapes, strawberries and peaches are always favorites. Try mixing fruits of one color: green grapes, kiwifruit and green apples or dark sweet cherries, red grapes and blueberries. Spoon into stemmed glasses or dessert dishes; garnish with a sprig of mint.

- Mix 1 cup dairy sour cream, 1 tablespoon plus 2 teaspoons packed brown sugar and 2 tablespoons amaretto. Serve over strawberries, blackberries or raspberries.

- Mix 1 cup dairy sour cream and 1 tablespoon packed brown sugar. Spoon over melon, mangoes, peaches or bananas; sprinkle with chopped crystallized ginger.

- Top slices of Almond-crusted Pound Cake (page 154) with fresh fruit and Hot Fudge Sauce (page 158) or sliced bananas and Amber Sauce (page 158).

Following pages: Almond-crusted Pound Cake with various toppings

Amber Sauce

½ cup packed brown sugar
¼ cup light corn syrup
¼ cup milk
2 tablespoons margarine or butter

Mix all ingredients in 1-quart saucepan. Cook over low heat, stirring occasionally, until sugar is dissolved and sauce is hot, about 5 minutes.

TO MICROWAVE: Decrease milk to 3 tablespoons. Mix all ingredients in 4-cup microwavable measure. Microwave uncovered on high (100%), stirring every minute, until sugar is dissolved, 2 to 3 minutes.

Hot Fudge Sauce

1 can (13 ounces) evaporated milk
1 package (12 ounces) semisweet chocolate chips
1 cup sugar
1 tablespoon margarine or butter
1 teaspoon vanilla

Heat milk, chips and sugar to boiling over medium heat, stirring constantly. Remove from heat; stir in margarine and vanilla. Serve warm. Store sauce in refrigerator up to 4 weeks.

TO MICROWAVE: Mix milk, chips and sugar in 4-cup microwavable measure. Microwave uncovered on medium (50%), stirring every 2 minutes, to boiling, 14 to 16 minutes; stir in margarine and vanilla.

Raspberry Currant Sauce

½ cup currant jelly
2 teaspoons cornstarch
1 cup fresh or loose pack frozen raspberries

Mix jelly and cornstarch in 1-quart saucepan; stir in raspberries. Heat to boiling, stirring constantly. Boil and stir 1 minute. Press through sieve to remove seeds. Cool at room temperature.

TO MICROWAVE: Mix jelly and cornstarch in 4-cup microwavable measure; stir in raspberries. Microwave uncovered on high (100%), stirring every minute, to boiling, 3 to 4 minutes. Continue as directed above.

Vanilla Custard Sauce

4 egg yolks, slightly beaten
¼ cup sugar
¼ teaspoon salt
1 cup milk
1 teaspoon vanilla

Mix egg yolks, sugar and salt in heavy 2-quart saucepan. Gradually stir in milk. Cook over low heat, stirring constantly, until mixture coats a metal spoon, about 30 minutes. (Do not boil; custard sauce will thicken slightly as it cools.)

Remove from heat; stir in vanilla. Place saucepan in cold water until sauce is cool. Cover and refrigerate at least 2 hours but no longer than 48 hours.

Rum Custard Sauce: Substitute 2 tablespoons rum for the vanilla.

TO MICROWAVE: Mix egg yolks, sugar and salt in 4-cup microwavable measure. Gradually stir in milk. Microwave uncovered on medium-high (70%) 3 minutes, stirring briskly every minute. Microwave uncovered, stirring every 30 seconds, until mixture coats a metal spoon and thickens slightly, 1 to 2 minutes longer. (Do not boil.) Stir in vanilla. Continue as directed above.

Fix It and Forget It

Main-dish Salads

Make-ahead salads are a cool way to handle humid August days. Not only do they save time—these salads benefit from being allowed to stand. The flavors in both Marinated Herbed Salmon and Broiled Sirloin and Mushroom Salad, for example, get a chance to mingle and come to life during refrigeration.

Wild Rice and Turkey Salad

4 SERVINGS

½ cup mayonnaise or salad dressing
¼ cup chutney
1 to 1½ teaspoons curry powder
½ teaspoon salt
3 cups cold cooked wild rice*
2 cups cut-up cooked turkey or chicken
2 cups broccoli flowerets

Mix mayonnaise, chutney, curry powder and salt in large bowl. Add wild rice, turkey and broccoli; toss. Cover and refrigerate at least 1 hour.

✱ 1 package (6¼ ounces) long grain and wild rice, prepared as directed on package and refrigerated until cold, can be substituted for the wild rice.

Wild Rice and Turkey Salad

Turkey and Apricot Salad

4 SERVINGS

2 cups cut-up cooked turkey or chicken
½ cup Coconut-Orange Dressing (below)
1 cup julienne jicama or 1 can (8 ounces) sliced
    water chestnuts, drained
1 package (6 ounces) dried apricots
2 large oranges, sectioned
2 medium carrots, coarsely shredded

Toss all ingredients. Cover and refrigerate until chilled, about 1 hour. Spoon onto salad greens if desired.

COCONUT-ORANGE DRESSING

1 can (9 ounces) cream of coconut
2 teaspoons grated orange peel
½ cup vegetable oil
¼ cup orange juice
½ teaspoon salt
¼ teaspoon curry powder

Stir all ingredients until thick. Cover and refrigerate until ready to serve. Stir before serving.

NOTE: Remaining dressing can be used for fruit salads or as a dip for fruit.

Pork and Apricot Salad: Substitute cooked pork for the turkey.

Hot Curried Chicken Salad

6 SERVINGS

2 cups cut-up cooked chicken or turkey
¾ cup mayonnaise or salad dressing
2 tablespoons finely chopped onion
2 tablespoons capers, drained
1 teaspoon curry powder
½ teaspoon salt
4 stalks celery, thinly sliced
½ cup toasted slivered almonds

Heat oven to 350°. Mix all ingredients except almonds. Spoon into ungreased 1-quart casserole or six 1-cup baking dishes. Sprinkle with almonds.

Bake uncovered until chicken mixture is hot, about 20 minutes.

TO MICROWAVE: Mix all ingredients except almonds. Spoon into 1-quart microwavable casserole. Cover loosely and microwave on medium (50%) 3 minutes; stir. Sprinkle with almonds. Cover loosely and microwave until hot, 4 to 7 minutes longer.

Turkey and Apricot Salad

Tuna and Tomato Salad

4 SERVINGS

¼ cup olive or vegetable oil
¼ cup wine vinegar
½ teaspoon red pepper sauce
2 medium tomatoes, coarsely chopped
1 bunch green onions (with tops), sliced
1 clove garlic, crushed
1 can (9¼ ounces) tuna, drained
½ pound fresh asparagus, cut diagonally into
   1-inch pieces*
6 cups bite-size pieces salad greens
Freshly ground pepper

Mix oil, vinegar, pepper sauce, tomatoes, onions, garlic and tuna in 4-quart bowl. Layer asparagus and salad greens on tuna mixture. Cover and refrigerate at least 2 hours but no longer than 24 hours. Sprinkle with pepper and toss just before serving.

✱ 2 cups chopped broccoli can be substituted for the asparagus.

Tuna and Cheddar Mold

4 SERVINGS

1 envelope unflavored gelatin
¾ cup cold water
¾ cup thinly sliced celery
½ cup shredded sharp Cheddar cheese
   (2 ounces)
⅓ cup mayonnaise, salad dressing or plain
   yogurt
¼ cup thinly sliced green onions (with tops)
¼ cup chopped green pepper
1 teaspoon lemon juice
½ teaspoon salt
½ teaspoon lemon pepper
1 can (9¼ ounces) tuna, drained
Salad greens

Sprinkle gelatin on cold water in 1½-quart saucepan to soften; heat over low heat, stirring constantly, until gelatin is dissolved. Remove from heat; stir in remaining ingredients except salad greens.

Pour into 4-cup mold. Refrigerate until firm; unmold. Garnish with salad greens.

Layered Tuna Salad

1 pared or unpared tart eating apple, cut into
  cubes
2 tablespoons lemon juice
3 cups bite-size pieces spinach (about 6 ounces)
1 can (9¼ ounces) tuna, drained
4 ounces bean sprouts
1 can (8½ ounces) sliced water chestnuts,
  drained
1 cup mayonnaise or salad dressing
2 tablespoons grated Parmesan cheese
1 tablespoon Chinese-style or Dijon-style mustard
1 teaspoon Worcestershire sauce
2 green onions (with tops), thinly sliced

Toss apple cubes and lemon juice. Place about half of the spinach in large glass bowl. Layer with tuna, apple, bean sprouts, remaining spinach and water chestnuts.

Mix remaining ingredients except onions; spread over water chestnuts, sealing to edge of bowl. Sprinkle with onions. Cover and refrigerate at least 2 hours but no longer than 24 hours.

Tuna and Cantaloupe Salad

1 package (6 ounces) frozen Chinese pea pods
2 cans (6½ ounces each) tuna, drained
3 cups cooked rice
⅓ cup mayonnaise or salad dressing
1 teaspoon instant chicken bouillon
¼ teaspoon ground ginger
3 small cantaloupe
⅓ cup salted cashews or peanuts, coarsely
  chopped

Rinse frozen pea pods in cold water to separate; drain. Mix pea pods, tuna, rice, mayonnaise, bouillon (dry) and ginger. Cover and refrigerate at least 2 hours.

Cut each cantaloupe crosswise into halves; scoop out seeds. (For decorative edge on shells, cut a saw-toothed or scalloped design.) Cut thin slice from bottom of each half to prevent tipping if necessary. Spoon about 1 cup tuna mixture into each half; sprinkle with cashews.

Greek Seafood Salad

¾ cup water

1 tablespoon margarine or butter

¼ teaspoon salt

½ cup uncooked couscous*

2 tablespoons snipped parsley

½ medium cucumber, chopped

4 medium radishes, chopped

1 package (6 ounces) frozen cooked shrimp, thawed, or 1½ cups cut-up cooked crabmeat

3 tablespoons olive or vegetable oil

2 tablespoons lemon juice

1 teaspoon salt

⅛ teaspoon pepper

½ cup whipping cream

1 teaspoon Dijon-style mustard

6 large tomatoes

Heat water, margarine and ¼ teaspoon salt to boiling in 1-quart saucepan; add couscous. Cover and remove from heat; let stand 5 minutes. Mix couscous, parsley, cucumber, radishes and shrimp in large bowl. Sprinkle with oil, lemon juice, 1 teaspoon salt and the pepper; stir until evenly coated. Cover and refrigerate until chilled, about 2 hours.

Beat whipping cream and mustard in chilled bowl until soft peaks form; stir into couscous mixture. Cut stem ends from tomatoes. Place tomatoes, cut sides down; cut each into sixths to within ½ inch of bottom. Carefully spread out sections. Fill with couscous mixture. Serve on lettuce leaves and garnish with additional parsley if desired.

Greek Poultry Salad: Substitute 1½ cups cut-up cooked chicken or turkey for the shrimp.

Greek Vegetable Salad: Omit shrimp. Use 1 medium cucumber and 8 medium radishes.

✳ 1½ cups cooked rice can be substituted for the cooked couscous.

Greek Seafood Salad

Seafood Salad with Dill Dressing

Creamy Dill Dressing (below)
1½ cups cooked medium shrimp (about ½ pound shelled)*
1 cup cut-up cooked crabmeat**
¼ cup sliced green onions (with tops)
1 medium cucumber, chopped
1 can (8½ ounces) sliced water chestnuts, drained
2 avocados, peeled and sliced
Salad greens

Prepare Creamy Dill Dressing; toss with remaining ingredients except avocados and salad greens. Cover and refrigerate at least 1 hour.

Arrange avocados on salad greens. Top with shrimp mixture.

* 1 package (6 ounces) frozen cooked medium shrimp, thawed, or 2 cans (4½ ounces each) large shrimp, drained, can be substituted for the fresh shrimp.

** 1 package (6 ounces) frozen cooked crabmeat, thawed, drained and cartilage removed, can be substituted for the fresh crabmeat.

CREAMY DILL DRESSING

½ cup mayonnaise or salad dressing
¼ cup dairy sour cream or plain yogurt
2 tablespoons lemon juice
1 teaspoon snipped fresh dill weed or ¼ teaspoon dried dill weed
¼ teaspoon salt

Mix all ingredients.

Seafood Salad with Dill Dressing

Marinated Herbed Salmon

1 teaspoon salt
¼ teaspoon dried dill weed
3 slices lemon
2 salmon steaks, each about 1 inch thick
1 small onion, thinly sliced
¼ cup wine vinegar
¼ teaspoon dried tarragon leaves
1 small cucumber
½ cup plain yogurt
¼ teaspoon salt
⅛ teaspoon dried dill weed
Lettuce leaves
2 medium tomatoes, sliced

Heat 1 inch water, 1 teaspoon salt, ¼ teaspoon dill weed and lemon slices to boiling in 10-inch skillet; reduce heat. Arrange salmon steaks in skillet. Simmer uncovered until salmon flakes easily with fork, 6 to 8 minutes; drain. Carefully remove skin from salmon.

Place salmon in shallow glass or plastic dish; arrange onion on salmon. Mix vinegar and tarragon; drizzle over onion and salmon. Cover and refrigerate at least 8 hours but no longer than 24 hours.

About 20 minutes before serving, cut cucumber lengthwise into halves; remove seeds. Cut halves crosswise into thin slices. Mix cucumber, yogurt, ¼ teaspoon salt and ⅛ teaspoon dill weed.

Place salmon on lettuce leaves; arrange onion and tomatoes around salmon. Drizzle any remaining marinade over salmon. Serve with cucumber mixture. Garnish with fresh dill weed if desired.

Easy Marinated Herbed Salmon: Substitute 1 can (15½ ounces) salmon, drained, for the salmon steaks; do not cook. Carefully separate salmon just enough to remove bones and skin. Top with onion and tarragon; pour vinegar over top. Cover and refrigerate at least 1 hour but no longer than 24 hours. Continue as directed above.

TO MICROWAVE: Omit water and decrease 1 teaspoon salt to ¼ teaspoon. Place salmon in square microwavable dish, 8 x 8 x 2 inches. Sprinkle with ¼ teaspoon salt and ¼ teaspoon dill weed. Arrange lemon slices on top.

Cover and microwave on high (100%) 3 minutes; rotate dish ½ turn. Microwave until small ends of salmon flake easily with fork, 3 to 6 minutes longer. Let stand covered 3 minutes; drain. Carefully remove skin from salmon and continue as directed above.

Creamy Mustard and Ham Mold

1 cup boiling water
1 package (3 ounces) lemon-flavored gelatin
1 tablespoon prepared mustard
1 package (3 ounces) cream cheese, softened
1 cup cold water
1 cup coarsely chopped fully cooked smoked ham
½ cup small pimiento-stuffed olives, well
   drained
1 stalk celery, thinly sliced
Salad greens

Pour boiling water on gelatin in bowl; stir until gelatin is dissolved. Stir mustard into cream cheese in medium bowl. Gradually stir gelatin into cream cheese mixture until well blended; stir in cold water. Refrigerate until slightly thickened.

Stir in ham, olives and celery. Pour into 4-cup mold or four 1-cup molds. Refrigerate until firm; unmold. Garnish with salad greens.

Beef Teriyaki Salad

½ cup mayonnaise or salad dressing
2 tablespoons teriyaki sauce
2 cups cooked rice
¾ pound cooked beef, cut into 2 x 1 x ⅛-inch
   pieces
4 ounces mushrooms, sliced, or 1 jar
   (2.5 ounces) sliced mushrooms, drained
4 ounces fresh Chinese pea pods or 1 package
   (6 ounces) frozen Chinese pea pods, thawed
   and drained
3 green onions (with tops), sliced

Mix mayonnaise and teriyaki sauce in large bowl. Add remaining ingredients; toss until coated. Cover and refrigerate at least 1 hour.

Broiled Sirloin and Mushroom Salad

1½-pound beef boneless sirloin steak, 1½ inches thick
1 jar (4.5 ounces) sliced mushrooms, drained
1 medium red or green pepper, cut into thin strips
⅓ cup red wine vinegar
¼ cup vegetable oil
1 teaspoon salt
1 teaspoon snipped fresh tarragon leaves or ¼ teaspoon dried tarragon leaves
½ teaspoon Worcestershire sauce
¼ teaspoon pepper
2 cloves garlic, crushed
Salad greens
Cherry or yellow pear tomatoes

Slash outer edge of fat on beef steak diagonally at 1-inch intervals to prevent curling (do not cut into lean). Set oven control to broil. Place beef on rack in broiler pan. Broil with top about 2 inches from heat until medium, about 13 minutes on each side. Cool beef; cut into ⅜-inch strips.

Arrange in ungreased rectangular baking dish, 13 x 9 x 2 inches. Place mushrooms on beef; top with pepper strips.

Mix remaining ingredients except salad greens and tomatoes; pour over beef and vegetables. Cover and refrigerate at least 3 hours, spooning marinade over vegetables occasionally.

Remove beef and vegetables with slotted spoon onto salad greens; garnish with tomatoes.

TO GRILL: Grill beef about 4 inches from hot coals until well done, 14 to 15 minutes on each side. Continue as directed above.

Broiled Sirloin and Mushroom Salad

Muffuletta Salad

Olive-Tomato Dressing (below)
2 cups uncooked mostaccioli
1 tablespoon olive oil
¼ pound sliced salami, cut into ⅛-inch strips
¼ pound thinly sliced fully cooked smoked ham, cut into ⅛-inch strips
¼ pound provolone cheese, cut into ⅛-inch strips
Salad greens

OLIVE-TOMATO DRESSING

1 anchovy fillet, mashed
1 large clove garlic, crushed
⅓ cup olive oil
1 cup cherry tomatoes, cut into halves
½ cup chopped pimiento-stuffed olives
½ cup chopped Greek or ripe olives
½ cup chopped mixed pickled vegetables
½ teaspoon dried oregano leaves

Prepare Olive-Tomato Dressing. Cook mostaccioli as directed on package; drain. Rinse in cold water; drain. Toss mostaccioli and oil.

Layer mostaccioli, salami, ham, provolone and salad greens on Olive-Tomato Dressing. Cover and refrigerate at least 4 hours but no longer than 24 hours. Toss just before serving. Arrange on salad greens.

Stir anchovy and garlic thoroughly into oil in large bowl. Stir in remaining ingredients.

Muffuletta Salad

Caesar Bean Salad

1 can (16 ounces) great northern beans, drained
1 can (15½ ounces) red kidney beans, drained
1 can (15 ounces) garbanzo beans, drained
½ cup sweet pickle relish
½ cup Caesar dressing
¼ cup snipped parsley
Salt and pepper to taste
Lemon wedges

Mix all ingredients except salt, pepper and lemon wedges in large bowl. Cover and refrigerate at least 1 hour, stirring occasionally.

Remove with slotted spoon and, if desired, arrange on salad greens; sprinkle with salt and pepper and, if desired, additional snipped parsley and grated Parmesan cheese. Garnish with lemon wedges.

Caesar Bean Salad with Avocados: For each salad, place avocado half on salad plate. Spoon about ½ cup bean mixture onto avocado.

Caesar Bean Salad with Tomatoes: For each salad, arrange 2 large slices tomato on salad plate. Spoon about ½ cup bean mixture onto tomato slices.

Salade Niçoise

Vinaigrette Dressing (below)
1 package (9 ounces) frozen whole or Italian-
    style green beans*
1 head Boston or leaf lettuce, torn into bite-size
    pieces
4 Italian plum tomatoes or 2 medium tomatoes,
    sliced
2 hard-cooked eggs, cut into fourths
1 can (9¼ ounces) tuna, drained
½ cup Greek or ripe olives
1 can (about 2 ounces) anchovy fillets
Snipped parsley

VINAIGRETTE DRESSING

½ cup olive or vegetable oil
¼ cup white wine vinegar
½ teaspoon salt
1½ teaspoons snipped fresh basil leaves or
    ½ teaspoon dried basil leaves
¼ teaspoon dry mustard
⅛ teaspoon pepper

Prepare Vinaigrette Dressing. Cook beans as directed on package; drain. Cover and refrigerate at least 1 hour.

Place lettuce on salad plates; arrange beans, tomatoes and eggs around edge. Mound tuna in center. Garnish with olives, anchovies and parsley. Serve with dressing and, if desired, with French Potato Salad (page 181) and crusty French bread.

✳ ¾ pound fresh green beans, cooked (about 2 cups), can be substituted for the frozen green beans.

Shake all ingredients in tightly covered container; refrigerate.

French Potato Salad

6 medium potatoes (about 2 pounds)
1/4 teaspoon instant beef or chicken bouillon
1/3 cup hot water
1/3 cup dry white wine
Tarragon Dressing (below)
3 tablespoons snipped parsley

Heat 1 inch salted water (1/2 teaspoon salt to 1 cup water) to boiling. Add potatoes. Heat to boiling; reduce heat. Cover and cook until tender, 30 to 35 minutes; drain and cool.

Cut potatoes into 1/4-inch slices. Place in glass or plastic bowl. Dissolve bouillon in hot water; add wine. Pour over potatoes. Cover and refrigerate, stirring occasionally, until cold, 3 to 4 hours but no longer than 24 hours.

Drain potatoes; toss with Tarragon Dressing until coated. Sprinkle with parsley. Serve with assorted cold meats or smoked fish and garnish with tomato wedges and deviled eggs if desired.

TARRAGON DRESSING

3 tablespoons olive or vegetable oil
2 tablespoons tarragon wine vinegar
2 teaspoons snipped chives
1 teaspoon salt
1 teaspoon Dijon-style mustard
1/2 teaspoon dried tarragon leaves
1/8 teaspoon pepper
1 clove garlic, cut into halves

Shake all ingredients in tightly covered container; discard garlic.

TO MICROWAVE: Cut potatoes into 1/4-inch slices. Place in 2-quart microwavable casserole. Cover tightly and microwave on high (100%) 5 minutes; stir. Cover tightly and microwave until tender, 6 to 8 minutes longer; drain. Dissolve bouillon in hot water; add wine. Pour over potato slices. Continue as directed above.

French Potato Salad (top) and Salade Niçoise

MAIN-DISH SALADS

Molded Egg Salad

2 envelopes unflavored gelatin
2 cups cold water
1 cup mayonnaise or salad dressing
2 tablespoons prepared mustard
1 teaspoon tarragon wine vinegar
6 hard-cooked eggs
1 cup cooked green peas
½ cup sliced radishes

Sprinkle gelatin on ½ cup of the cold water in 1-quart saucepan to soften. Heat over low heat, stirring constantly, until gelatin is dissolved; pour into large bowl. Stir in remaining cold water, the mayonnaise, mustard and vinegar; beat until smooth. Refrigerate until slightly thickened.

Slice 2 eggs; arrange in single layer on bottom of 5-cup mold. Slice remaining eggs; stir eggs, peas and radishes into gelatin mixture. Pour over eggs in mold. Refrigerate until firm; unmold. Serve with assorted luncheon meats if desired.

Pesto Macaroni Salad

3 cups uncooked medium shell macaroni
1 tablespoon olive or vegetable oil
1 container (8 ounces) pesto or 1 cup Pesto
  (page 144)
4 Italian plum tomatoes, each cut into 4 wedges
½ cup small pitted ripe olives
¼ cup white wine vinegar
4 cups coarsely shredded spinach
Grated Parmesan cheese

Cook macaroni as directed on package; drain. Rinse in cold water; drain and toss with oil.

Mix pesto, tomatoes, olives and vinegar in large bowl. Arrange 2 cups of the macaroni and 2 cups of the spinach on pesto mixture; repeat with remaining macaroni and spinach. Cover and refrigerate at least 2 hours but no longer than 24 hours. Toss; sprinkle with cheese.

Pesto, Macaroni and Shrimp Salad: Add 1 package (6 ounces) frozen cooked tiny shrimp, thawed, just before tossing.

Pesto, Macaroni and Tuna Salad: Add 1 can (6½ ounces) tuna, drained, just before tossing.

Molded Egg Salad

Soups and Stews

After work or after school, nothing whets an appetite like the aroma of soup. The beauty of these recipes is their simplicity: Combine the ingredients in a Dutch oven and simmer for a couple of hours while you relax. For those days when time is especially tight, many of the dishes have microwave instructions.

Chicken and Bean Soup with Parsley

8 SERVINGS

8 cups water
1 cup dried great northern beans
1 cup dried kidney beans
1 teaspoon rubbed sage
1 package (2.5 ounces) onion soup mix
  (2 envelopes)
2 whole boneless skinless chicken breasts, cut into
  1-inch pieces (about 1 pound)
½ cup snipped parsley

Heat water, beans, sage and soup mix (dry) to boiling in 4-quart Dutch oven. Boil 2 minutes; reduce heat. Cover and simmer until beans are tender, about 2½ hours.

Stir in chicken and parsley. Cover and cook until chicken is done, about 15 minutes.

Chicken and Bean Soup with Parsley

Turkey and Wild Rice Soup

½ cup uncooked wild rice
3½ cups water
1 tablespoon instant chicken bouillon (dry)
2 turkey drumsticks (about 1½ pounds)
2 medium stalks celery (with leaves), sliced
1 medium onion, chopped
2 bay leaves
1 can (16 ounces) stewed tomatoes

Mix all ingredients in 4-quart Dutch oven. Heat to boiling; reduce heat. Cover and simmer until turkey is done and wild rice is tender, 50 to 60 minutes.

Remove turkey drumsticks; cool about 5 minutes. Remove skin and bones from turkey; cut turkey into bite-size pieces. Stir turkey into soup. Heat until hot. Remove bay leaves.

TO MICROWAVE: Decrease water to 3 cups and use hot water. Mix all ingredients in 3-quart microwavable casserole. Cover tightly and microwave on high (100%), turning drumsticks over every 10 minutes, until turkey is done, 30 to 40 minutes. Remove turkey; cool about 5 minutes.

Cover wild rice mixture tightly and microwave until wild rice is tender, 8 to 10 minutes longer. Remove skin and bones from turkey; cut turkey into bite-size pieces. Stir turkey into soup. Cover tightly and microwave until hot, 2 to 3 minutes. Remove bay leaves.

Beef and Pinto Bean Stew

1 cup dried pinto beans
5 cups water
1 pound beef boneless chuck, tip or round roast,
*   cut into ½-inch pieces*
¼ cup packed brown sugar
1 teaspoon salt
½ teaspoon dry mustard
¼ teaspoon ground cinnamon
¼ teaspoon pepper
1 large onion, chopped
1 can (6 ounces) tomato paste

Heat beans and water to boiling in 4-quart oven-proof Dutch oven. Boil 2 minutes. Stir remaining ingredients into bean mixture. Cover and bake in 325° oven 2 hours; stir. Cover and bake until beef and beans are tender, about 2 hours longer.

Red Wine Beef Stew

1/4 pound salt pork
1 1/2 pounds beef boneless chuck, tip or round
    steak, cut into 1-inch pieces
1 cup dry red wine
1/2 cup water
1/2 teaspoon salt
1/2 teaspoon dried thyme leaves
1/4 teaspoon dried rosemary leaves
1/4 teaspoon pepper
2 cloves garlic, chopped
1 bay leaf
6 carrots, cut into 1-inch pieces
2 medium onions, cut into fourths
1/2 cup pitted ripe olives
Snipped parsley

Remove rind from salt pork; cut pork into 1/4-inch slices. Cook salt pork in 4-quart Dutch oven over medium heat until crisp. Remove with slotted spoon; drain.

Cook and stir beef in hot fat until brown, about 15 minutes; drain fat. Add wine, water, salt, and seasonings to Dutch oven. Heat to boiling; reduce heat. Cover and simmer 1 hour.

Stir in salt pork, carrots, onions and olives. Cover and simmer until beef and vegetables are tender, about 40 minutes. Remove bay leaf. Sprinkle with parsley.

TO MICROWAVE: Omit water. Cut beef into 1/2-inch cubes. Place salt pork and beef in 3-quart microwavable casserole. Cover tightly and microwave on high (100%) 5 minutes; stir. Cover tightly and microwave until almost no pink remains, 3 to 5 minutes longer. Remove salt pork; reserve.

Add wine, salt and seasonings to beef. Cover tightly and microwave on medium-low (30%) 20 minutes; stir. Cover tightly and microwave 20 minutes longer. Add salt pork, carrots, onions and olives. Cover tightly and microwave on medium (50%) 10 minutes; stir. Cover tightly and microwave until carrots are tender, 10 to 15 minutes longer. Remove bay leaf. Sprinkle with parsley.

Following pages: Beef Stew with Chutney

SOUPS AND STEWS

Beef Stew with Chutney

1½-pound beef boneless chuck, tip or round
    roast, cut into 1-inch pieces
2 tablespoons olive or vegetable oil
½ cup chutney
1 cup apple juice or water
1 tablespoon curry powder
2 medium tomatoes, chopped
1 large onion, sliced
1 small butternut squash, cut into cubes
Hot cooked bulgur or rice

Cook and stir beef in oil in 4-quart Dutch oven or 12-inch skillet until brown, about 15 minutes; drain. Stir in remaining ingredients except squash and bulgur. Heat to boiling; reduce heat. Cover and simmer until beef is almost tender, about 2 hours.

Stir in squash; cover and cook until beef and squash are tender, about 15 minutes. Serve with bulgur and, if desired, additional chutney and chopped cilantro.

TO MICROWAVE: Cut beef into ½-inch pieces. Omit oil; decrease apple juice to ½ cup and curry powder to 2 teaspoons. Place beef and onion in 3-quart microwavable casserole. Cover tightly and microwave on high (100%) 6 minutes; stir. Cover tightly and microwave until beef is no longer pink, 6 to 8 minutes longer (do not drain).

Stir in remaining ingredients except squash, bulgur and cilantro. Cover tightly and microwave to boiling, 4 to 6 minutes; stir. Cover tightly and microwave on medium-low (30%) 15 minutes; stir. Cover tightly and microwave 15 minutes longer. Stir in squash. Cover tightly and microwave until beef and squash are tender, 15 to 20 minutes. Serve as directed above.

Chunky Beef Noodle Soup

1 pound beef boneless round steak, cut into
  ¾-inch pieces
1 large onion, chopped
2 cloves garlic, finely chopped
1 tablespoon vegetable oil
2 cups water
2 teaspoons chili powder
1½ teaspoons salt
½ teaspoon dried oregano leaves
1 can (16 ounces) whole tomatoes, undrained
1 can (10½ ounces) condensed beef broth
2 ounces uncooked egg noodles (about 1 cup)
1 medium green pepper, coarsely chopped
¼ cup snipped parsley

Cook and stir beef steak, onion and garlic in oil in 4-quart Dutch oven until beef is brown, about 15 minutes. Stir in water, chili powder, salt, oregano, tomatoes and broth; break up tomatoes. Heat to boiling; reduce heat. Cover and simmer until beef is tender, 1½ to 2 hours.

Skim excess fat from soup. Stir noodles and green pepper into soup. Heat to boiling; reduce heat. Simmer uncovered until noodles are tender, about 10 minutes. Stir in parsley.

TO MICROWAVE: Cut beef steak into ½-inch pieces. Omit oil. Decrease water to 1½ cups. Place beef, onion and garlic in 3-quart microwavable casserole. Cover tightly and microwave on high (100%) 4 minutes; stir. Cover tightly and microwave until very little pink remains in beef, 2 to 4 minutes longer.

Stir in water, chili powder, salt, oregano, tomatoes and broth; break up tomatoes. Cover tightly and microwave to boiling, 6 to 10 minutes; stir. Cover tightly and microwave on medium (50%) 30 minutes; stir. Cover tightly and microwave until beef is tender, 25 to 30 minutes longer.

Stir noodles and green pepper into soup. Cover tightly and microwave until noodles are tender, 9 to 12 minutes. Stir in parsley.

Sauerbraten-style Stew

1 pound beef boneless chuck or round steak, cut
    into 1-inch pieces
1 teaspoon salt
1/4 teaspoon ground cloves
1/4 teaspoon pepper
1 1/2 cups water
1/4 cup red wine vinegar
1 can (10 1/2 ounces) condensed beef broth
1 bay leaf
1 medium onion, chopped
1/2 small head red cabbage, coarsely shredded
8 gingersnaps, crushed (about 1/2 cup)
1 tablespoon packed brown sugar

Mix all ingredients except gingersnaps and brown sugar in 4-quart ovenproof Dutch oven. Cover and bake in 325° oven until beef is tender, about 2 hours.

Remove bay leaf. Stir gingersnaps and brown sugar into stew. Cover and bake 10 minutes. Serve with hot buttered poppy seed noodles if desired.

TO MICROWAVE: Cut beef into 1/2-inch pieces. Decrease water to 1 1/4 cups and vinegar to 2 tablespoons. Mix all ingredients except vinegar, gingersnaps and brown sugar in 3-quart microwavable casserole. Cover tightly and microwave on high (100%) to boiling, 10 to 12 minutes; stir. Cover tightly and microwave on medium (50%), stirring every 15 minutes, until beef is tender, 35 to 45 minutes longer. Remove bay leaf.

Stir in vinegar, gingersnaps and brown sugar. Cover tightly and microwave on high (100%) until mixture thickens and boils, 3 to 4 minutes. Serve as directed above.

Baked Chili

1 1/2 cups dried pinto beans
6 cups water
1 1/2 pounds beef boneless chuck, tip or round
    steak, cut into 1-inch pieces
3 tablespoons chili powder
1 tablespoon cumin seed
1 1/2 teaspoons salt
1 1/2 teaspoons ground red pepper
3 medium onions, chopped
3 cloves garlic, finely chopped
3 cans (8 ounces each) tomato sauce

Heat beans and water to boiling in 4-quart ovenproof Dutch oven. Boil 2 minutes.

Stir remaining ingredients into bean mixture. Cover and bake in 325° oven until beef and beans are tender, about 4 hours; stir. Garnish with dairy sour cream, chopped onion and shredded Cheddar cheese if desired.

Red Summer Soup

1 cup water
1 can (16 ounces) julienne beets, drained
    (reserve liquid)
1 small head red cabbage (about 1 pound),
    coarsely shredded
1 package (10 ounces) frozen raspberries in
    juice, undrained
1 tablespoon lemon juice
Plain yogurt

Heat water, beet liquid and cabbage to boiling in 3-quart saucepan; reduce heat. Cover and simmer until cabbage is very tender, about 1 hour.

Carefully pour cabbage mixture and raspberries into workbowl of food processor fitted with steel blade or into blender container. Cover and process until smooth.

Return mixture to saucepan; stir in beets and lemon juice. Heat over medium heat, stirring occasionally, until hot. Garnish with yogurt and, if desired, lemon peel.

Chilled Red Summer Soup: After stirring in beets and lemon juice, cover and refrigerate until completely chilled, at least 4 hours but no longer than 24 hours. Stir before serving.

Braised Rabbit Stew

2 tablespoons margarine or butter
2½- to 3-pound domestic rabbit, cut up
1 teaspoon salt
1 teaspoon snipped fresh rosemary leaves or
    ½ teaspoon dried rosemary leaves, crushed
¼ teaspoon pepper
1 bay leaf
¼ cup quick-cooking tapioca
6 medium carrots, cut crosswise into 1-inch
    pieces
1 jar (16 ounces) small whole onions
3 cups water
¾ cup dry red wine or chicken broth
½ teaspoon browning sauce

Heat margarine in 4-quart Dutch oven until melted. Arrange rabbit in Dutch oven. Sprinkle with salt, rosemary, pepper, bay leaf and tapioca. Add carrots and onions. Mix water, wine and browning sauce; pour over rabbit and vegetables.

Cover and bake in 325° oven until rabbit is tender, about 2½ hours. Remove rabbit from bones if desired. Return rabbit to broth; stir. Remove bay leaf.

Following pages: Sauerbraten-style Stew (left) and Red Summer Soup

Lamb and Barley Stew

2 pounds lamb boneless shoulder, cut into 1-inch
   pieces
1 teaspoon salt
2 teaspoons snipped fresh rosemary leaves or
   ¾ teaspoon dried rosemary leaves, crushed
¼ teaspoon pepper
2 cloves garlic, finely chopped
½ cup uncooked barley
1 medium onion, chopped
4 medium carrots, cut into 1-inch pieces
2 cups water

Place lamb in 4-quart Dutch oven. Sprinkle with salt, rosemary, pepper and garlic.

Layer barley, onion and carrots on top. Pour water over carrots. Cover and bake in 325° oven until lamb and barley are tender, about 2 hours.

TO MICROWAVE: Cut lamb into ½-inch pieces and carrots into ½-inch slices. Decrease water to 1¾ cups and use hot water.

Place lamb in 3-quart microwavable casserole. Cover tightly and microwave on high (100%) 6 minutes; stir. Cover tightly and microwave until no longer pink, 6 to 8 minutes longer (do not drain).

Stir in remaining ingredients. Cover tightly and microwave to boiling, 8 to 10 minutes; stir. Cover tightly and microwave on medium-low (30%), stirring every 15 minutes, until barley is tender, 40 to 50 minutes longer.

Irish Lamb Stew

2 pounds lamb boneless neck or shoulder, cut
   into 1-inch pieces
6 medium potatoes, cut into ½-inch slices (about
   2 pounds)
3 medium onions, sliced
2 teaspoons salt
¼ teaspoon pepper
2 cups water
Snipped parsley

Layer half each of the lamb, potatoes and onions in 4-quart Dutch oven; sprinkle with half each of the salt and pepper. Repeat; add water.

Heat to boiling; reduce heat. Cover and simmer until lamb is tender, 1½ to 2 hours. Skim fat from broth (see note). Sprinkle stew with parsley. Serve in bowls with pickled red cabbage if desired.

NOTE: To remove fat easily, prepare stew the day before, cover and refrigerate. Remove fat before reheating.

TO MICROWAVE: Cut lamb into ½-inch pieces. Cut potatoes into ¼-inch slices. Omit water. Place lamb in 3-quart microwavable casserole. Cover tightly and microwave on high (100%) 6 minutes; stir. Cover tightly and microwave until very little pink remains, 6 to 9 minutes longer. Drain, reserving ½ cup drippings.

Arrange potatoes in square microwavable dish, 8 x 8 x 2 inches; sprinkle with 2 tablespoons water. Cover tightly and microwave on high (100%) until barely tender, 8 to 12 minutes.

Add potatoes, onions, salt and pepper to lamb in 3-quart casserole; stir. Pour reserved drippings over top. Cover tightly and microwave on medium-low (30%) 20 minutes; stir. Cover tightly and microwave until lamb is tender, 20 to 28 minutes longer. Continue as directed above.

Hoppin' John Soup

½ pound dried black-eyed peas or dried red
  beans (about 1 cup)
8 cups water
½ to 1 teaspoon very finely chopped jalapeño or
  other hot chili pepper or ¼ to ½ teaspoon
  crushed red pepper
1 clove garlic, finely chopped
1 ham bone or 1 pound ham shank or smoked
  pork hocks
½ cup uncooked long-grain regular rice
2 medium onions, chopped
1 red or green bell pepper, chopped
1 teaspoon salt
¼ teaspoon pepper
8 ounces Swiss chard or mustard greens, coarsely
  chopped (about 4 cups)

Heat peas and water to boiling in 4-quart Dutch oven; boil uncovered 2 minutes. Remove from heat; cover and let stand 1 hour.

Stir in jalapeño, garlic and ham bone. Heat to boiling; reduce heat. Cover and simmer until peas are tender, 1 to 1½ hours (do not boil or peas will burst).

Remove ham bone; trim ham from bone and reserve. Stir rice, onions, bell pepper, salt and pepper into Dutch oven. Cover and simmer, stirring occasionally, until rice is tender, about 25 minutes. Stir in ham and Swiss chard; cover and simmer until heated through.

Lentil Soup with Asparagus and Gruyère

1 cup dried lentils
4 cups water
1 tablespoon instant chicken bouillon (dry)
½ teaspoon lemon and pepper seasoning salt
1 small onion, chopped
1 stalk celery (with leaves), sliced
¾ pound fresh asparagus, cut into ½-inch
  pieces, or 1 package (10 ounces) frozen
  asparagus cuts
1 cup shredded Gruyère or Swiss cheese
  (4 ounces)
Dairy sour cream

Mix all ingredients except cheese and sour cream in 4-quart Dutch oven. Heat to boiling; reduce heat. Cover and simmer until lentils are very tender, about 45 minutes.

Remove 1 cup of the vegetables with slotted spoon; reserve. Carefully pour remaining hot mixture into workbowl of food processor fitted with steel blade or into blender container. Cover and process until smooth.

Mix processed mixture, reserved vegetables and the cheese in Dutch oven. Heat over medium heat, stirring constantly, until cheese is melted and mixture is hot. Garnish each serving with dollop of sour cream.

Hoppin' John Soup

Lentil and Brown Rice Soup

3/4 cup dried lentils

1/2 cup uncooked brown or regular rice

6 cups water

1/2 teaspoon ground cumin

1/2 teaspoon salt

1/4 teaspoon pepper

1/2 package (2.5-ounce size) onion soup mix
    (1 envelope)

3 ounces spinach, cut into 1/2-inch strips
    (about 1 cup)

2 tablespoons snipped cilantro or parsley

3 tablespoons lemon juice

Heat lentils, rice, water, cumin, salt, pepper and soup mix (dry) to boiling in 4-quart Dutch oven; reduce heat. Cover and simmer, stirring occasionally, until lentils are tender, about 40 minutes.

Stir in spinach, cilantro and lemon juice until spinach is wilted. Serve with additional snipped cilantro and lemon slices if desired.

Cauliflower and Cheese Soup

5 SERVINGS

2 cups water

1 small head cauliflower (about 1 pound),
    broken into large flowerets, or 2 packages
    (8 ounces each) frozen cauliflower

1 medium stalk celery, cut into 1/2-inch pieces

1 medium carrot, cut into 1/2-inch pieces

1 small onion, cut into eighths

1 tablespoon instant chicken bouillon (dry)

1/4 teaspoon lemon and pepper seasoning salt

1 can (5 ounces) evaporated milk

1 1/2 cups shredded Havarti or Monterey Jack
    cheese (6 ounces)

Cover and cook all ingredients except milk and cheese in 3-quart saucepan over medium-low heat until vegetables are very tender, about 1 1/2 hours.

Carefully pour mixture into workbowl of food processor fitted with steel blade or into blender container. Cover and process until smooth.

Return mixture to saucepan; stir in milk and cheese. Heat over medium heat, stirring constantly, until cheese is melted and mixture is hot.

Lentil and Brown Rice Soup

Cream of Squash Soup

1 small onion, chopped
2 tablespoons margarine or butter
2 packages (12 ounces each) frozen cooked
  squash
1 can (10¾ ounces) condensed chicken broth
½ teaspoon salt
¼ teaspoon ground nutmeg
Dash of pepper
½ cup whipping cream

Cook and stir onion in margarine in 3-quart saucepan until tender. Stir in remaining ingredients except whipping cream.

Cover and cook over low heat until squash is hot, 45 to 50 minutes. Stir in whipping cream; heat until hot. Garnish with toasted nuts if desired.

TO MICROWAVE: Place onion and margarine in 3-quart microwavable casserole. Cover tightly and microwave on high (100%) until margarine is melted and bubbly, about 3 minutes.

Unwrap frozen blocks of squash and place side by side on margarine mixture in casserole; add remaining ingredients except whipping cream. Cover tightly and microwave until squash is partially thawed, 5 to 6 minutes; break up squash with fork. Cover tightly and microwave 5 minutes; stir. Cover tightly and microwave to boiling, 5 to 7 minutes longer. Stir in whipping cream. Cover tightly and microwave until hot, 2 to 4 minutes.

Golden Onion Soup

Parmesan Croutons (below)
1/4 cup margarine or butter
1 tablespoon packed brown sugar
1 teaspoon Worcestershire sauce
2 large onions (3/4 to 1 pound each), cut into fourths and sliced
2 cans (10 1/2 ounces each) condensed beef broth
2 soup cans water

PARMESAN CROUTONS

1/4 cup margarine or butter
3 slices bread, cut into 1-inch cubes
Grated Parmesan cheese

Prepare Parmesan Croutons; reserve. Reduce oven temperature to 325°. Heat margarine in 4-quart ovenproof Dutch oven until melted; stir in brown sugar and Worcestershire sauce. Toss onions in margarine mixture.

Bake uncovered, stirring every hour, until onions are deep golden brown, about 2 1/2 hours. Stir in broth and water; heat to boiling over high heat. Serve with Parmesan Croutons.

Heat oven to 400°. Heat margarine in rectangular pan, 13 x 9 x 2 inches, in oven until melted. Toss bread cubes in margarine until evenly coated. Sprinkle with cheese. Bake uncovered, stirring occasionally, until golden brown and crisp, 10 to 15 minutes.

Golden Onion Soup with Mozzarella: Spoon soup into ovenproof bowls; top with croutons. Sprinkle each serving with 1/4 cup shredded mozzarella cheese. Place bowls in oven until cheese is melted.

Following pages: Golden Onion Soup with Mozzarella

Eggs and Cheese

When it comes to leisurely weekend meals, mellow eggs and cheese are a match made in heaven. Take our delectable Crabmeat Strata, for example. Minimal preparation time the night before and a trip to the oven the next day yield a brunch or supper entrée just right for six hearty appetites.

Potatoes and Eggs Sunny-side Up

12 ounces bulk pork sausage
1 small onion, chopped
3 cups frozen shredded hash brown potatoes
1 teaspoon herb-seasoned salt
1½ cups shredded Swiss cheese (6 ounces)
6 eggs

Heat oven to 350°. Cook and stir sausage and onion in 10-inch skillet over medium heat until sausage is brown; drain. Stir in frozen potatoes and herb-seasoned salt. Cook, stirring constantly, just until potatoes are thawed, about 2 minutes. Remove from heat; stir in cheese. Spread in ungreased rectangular baking dish, 11 x 7 x 1½ inches.

Make 6 indentations in potato mixture with back of spoon; break 1 egg into each indentation. Sprinkle with pepper if desired. Bake uncovered until eggs are desired doneness, 20 to 25 minutes.

Potatoes and Egg Sunny-side Up

Cheese and Egg Pie with Bacon

1 cup coarsely crushed cornflakes
2 tablespoons margarine or butter, melted
1/4 cup margarine or butter
8 eggs
1/2 cup milk
1 tablespoon snipped chives
1/2 teaspoon seasoned salt
1/8 teaspoon pepper
6 slices bacon, crisply cooked and crumbled
3 slices process American cheese, cut diagonally
  into halves

Mix cornflakes and melted margarine; reserve 1/4 cup. Spread remaining cornflake mixture in ungreased pie plate, 9 x 1 1/4 inches, or quiche dish, 9 x 1 1/2 inches. Heat 1/4 cup margarine in 10-inch skillet over medium heat until melted.

Beat eggs, milk, chives, seasoned salt and pepper with hand beater. Pour egg mixture into skillet; add bacon. Cook over low heat, stirring gently, until eggs are almost set. Quickly spoon into pie plate. Arrange cheese, overlapping slightly, around edge of plate. Sprinkle with reserved cornflake mixture. Bake uncovered in 375° oven until cheese is melted and eggs are firm, 10 to 15 minutes.

TO MICROWAVE: Mix cornflakes and melted margarine; reserve 1/4 cup. Spread remaining cornflake mixture in microwavable pie plate, 9 x 1 1/4 inches. Omit 1/4 cup margarine. Mix eggs, milk, chives, seasoned salt and pepper with hand beater in 1 1/2-quart microwavable casserole; stir in bacon. Cover tightly and microwave on high (100%), stirring every 2 minutes, until eggs are puffy and set but still moist, 6 to 8 minutes.

Quickly spoon into pie plate. Arrange cheese, overlapping slightly, around edge of plate; sprinkle with reserved mixture. Microwave uncovered on medium (50%) until cheese is melted, 2 to 3 minutes.

Cheese and Egg Pie with Bacon

Baked Vegetable Omelet

1 cup shredded pepper Jack cheese (4 ounces)
1½ cups chopped broccoli or 1 package
    (10 ounces) frozen chopped broccoli, thawed
    and drained
2 medium tomatoes, coarsely chopped
2 cups shredded Cheddar cheese (8 ounces)
1 cup milk
¼ cup all-purpose flour
½ teaspoon salt
3 eggs

Layer pepper cheese, broccoli, tomatoes and Cheddar cheese in ungreased square baking dish, 8 x 8 x 2 inches. Beat milk, flour, salt and eggs until smooth; pour over cheese.

Bake uncovered in 350° oven until egg mixture is set, 40 to 45 minutes. Let stand 10 minutes before cutting.

Baked Eggs and Artichokes

8 SERVINGS

1 package (6 ounces) toasted croutons (4 cups)
8 hard-cooked eggs, cut into halves
1 can (14 ounces) artichoke hearts, drained and
    cut into fourths
1 can (10¾ ounces) condensed cream of chicken
    soup
½ soup can milk
¼ cup dry white wine
1 teaspoon dry mustard
1½ cups shredded Swiss cheese (6 ounces)
6 slices bacon, crisply cooked and crumbled

Place croutons in ungreased rectangular baking dish, 11 x 7 x 1½ inches. Arrange eggs and artichoke hearts on croutons.

Mix soup, milk, wine and mustard in 1½-quart saucepan; heat to boiling, stirring frequently. Remove from heat; stir in cheese until melted. Pour evenly over eggs and artichoke hearts; sprinkle with bacon. Bake uncovered in 350° oven until hot and bubbly, about 30 minutes.

Baked Vegetable Omelet

Ham and Cheddar Strata

12 slices bread
2 cups cut-up fully cooked smoked ham
2 cups shredded Cheddar cheese (8 ounces)
1 bunch green onions (with tops), sliced
2 cups milk
1 teaspoon dry mustard
1/4 teaspoon red pepper sauce
6 eggs
Paprika

Trim crusts from bread. Arrange 6 slices bread in greased rectangular baking dish, 13 x 9 x 2 inches. Layer ham, cheese and onions on bread in dish. Cut remaining bread slices diagonally into halves; arrange on onions.

Beat milk, mustard, pepper sauce and eggs until smooth; pour evenly over bread. Sprinkle with paprika. Bake immediately, or cover and refrigerate up to 24 hours.

Heat oven to 300°. Bake uncovered until center is set and bread is golden brown, 60 to 70 minutes. Let stand 10 minutes before cutting.

Baked Ham and Brie with Pears

6 SERVINGS

1/4 cup milk
1 tablespoon margarine or butter, melted
1 egg
4 slices rye bread, cut into cubes
1/2 pound fully cooked smoked ham, coarsely
    chopped
2 small pears, thinly sliced
8 ounces Brie cheese, cut into cubes

Beat milk, margarine and egg. Toss with bread cubes. Turn into ungreased square baking dish, 8 x 8 x 2 inches. Top with ham, pears and cheese.

Bake uncovered in 350° oven until pears are tender and cheese is melted, 25 to 30 minutes.

Ham and Cheddar Strata

Eggs and Broccoli with Cheddar Sauce

1 package (10 ounces) frozen chopped broccoli
1/2 teaspoon salt
12 hard-cooked eggs, cut lengthwise into fourths
3/4 cup milk
1 teaspoon parsley flakes
1/2 teaspoon dry mustard
1/4 teaspoon dried basil leaves
1/8 teaspoon onion powder
3 drops red pepper sauce
1 can (11 ounces) condensed Cheddar cheese
    soup
1 jar (2 ounces) diced pimientos, drained
1 cup crushed corn chips or potato chips

Rinse broccoli in cold water to separate; drain. Spread broccoli in ungreased rectangular baking dish, 12 x 7 1/2 x 2 inches; sprinkle with salt. Arrange eggs, cut sides up, on broccoli.

Mix remaining ingredients except corn chips in saucepan; heat to boiling. Pour evenly over eggs; sprinkle with chips. Bake uncovered in 350° oven until hot, 20 to 25 minutes.

Crabmeat Strata

1 package (6 ounces) plain croutons
1 1/2 cups shredded Gruyère or Swiss cheese
    (6 ounces)
1 package (8 ounces) frozen imitation crabmeat,
    thawed and cut up
6 green onions (with tops), sliced
1 1/2 cups milk
1/2 teaspoon dry mustard
4 eggs

Arrange half of the croutons in greased square baking dish, 8 x 8 x 2 inches; layer with cheese, crabmeat, onions and remaining croutons. Beat milk, mustard and eggs; pour evenly over croutons. Cover and refrigerate at least 2 hours but no longer than 24 hours.

Heat oven to 300°. Bake uncovered until knife inserted in center comes out clean, 55 to 60 minutes. Let stand 10 minutes before cutting.

Double Cheese and Potato Casserole

6 SERVINGS

2 cups shredded Cheddar cheese (8 ounces)
5 eggs
1 cup small curd creamed cottage cheese
1 1/2 cups water
1 cup milk
1 teaspoon dry mustard
1/2 teaspoon salt
1/4 teaspoon red pepper sauce
1 bunch green onions (with tops), sliced
1 package (6 ounces) hash brown potatoes (dry)

Heat oven to 350°. Reserve 1 cup of the Cheddar cheese. Beat eggs in ungreased rectangular baking dish, 12 x 7 1/2 x 2 inches; beat in remaining ingredients. Sprinkle with reserved Cheddar cheese.

Bake uncovered until knife inserted in center comes out clean, 40 to 45 minutes.

Green and Gold Soufflé

5 SERVINGS

1 package (12 ounces) frozen spinach soufflé
1 package (12 ounces) frozen corn soufflé
6 ounces Swiss cheese, cut into 1/2-inch cubes

Heat oven to 350°. Butter 6-cup soufflé dish. Remove frozen soufflés from foil pans. Cut each soufflé into 1-inch squares. Mix soufflé squares and cheese in dish.

Bake uncovered until knife inserted in center comes out clean, 75 to 80 minutes.

Nacho Cheese Puff

1 can (11 ounces) condensed nacho cheese soup
6 eggs, separated
¼ teaspoon cream of tartar

Heat oven to 350°. Butter 2-quart casserole or souf-flé dish. Heat soup to boiling over medium heat, stirring constantly; remove from heat. Beat egg whites and cream of tartar in large bowl until stiff but not dry. Beat egg yolks slightly; stir into soup.

Stir about ¼ of the egg white mixture into soup mixture. Fold soup mixture into remaining egg white mixture. Carefully pour into casserole. Bake uncovered until knife inserted halfway between center and edge comes out clean, 50 to 60 minutes. Serve immediately.

Individual Nacho Cheese Puffs: Butter six 10-ounce custard cups. Divide mixture evenly among cups; place cups on cookie sheet. Bake 25 to 30 minutes.

Individual Nacho Cheese Puff

Grains and Pasta

If you love homey baked pasta dishes but seldom have time to make them, you'll be delighted with our innovative shortcuts for some favorite recipes. By not precooking the noodles, we have developed almost effortless versions of Vegetable Lasagne, regular Cheesy Lasagne and Manicotti.

Baked Broccoli and Chili Beans

6 SERVINGS

1 cup uncooked instant rice
2 cans (16 ounces each) hot chili beans,
*   undrained*
1 package (16 ounces) frozen cut broccoli
6 slices bacon, crisply cooked and crumbled
8 ounces Mexican-style process cheese spread
*   loaf, cut into cubes*

Mix all ingredients except cheese in ungreased 3-quart casserole; sprinkle with cheese.

Cover and bake in 350° oven until rice and broccoli are tender, about 1 hour.

TO MICROWAVE: Cut uncooked bacon into 1-inch pieces. Place bacon in 3-quart microwavable casserole. Cover with waxed paper and microwave on high (100%) 3 minutes; stir. Cover with waxed paper and microwave until bacon is crisp, 3 to 4 minutes longer; drain, reserving bacon in casserole.

Stir remaining ingredients except cheese into casserole. Cover tightly and microwave 10 minutes; stir. Cover tightly and microwave 4 minutes; stir. Cover tightly and microwave until rice and broccoli are tender, 4 to 6 minutes longer. Arrange cheese on top; microwave uncovered until cheese is melted, 2 to 3 minutes.

Baked Broccoli and Chili Beans

Spicy Chicken and Brown Rice

2 cups cut-up cooked chicken or turkey
1 cup uncooked brown rice
½ cup currants or raisins
2½ cups boiling water
1 teaspoon salt
½ teaspoon ground cinnamon
¼ teaspoon ground cloves
1 small onion, chopped
1 can (10¾ ounces) condensed cream of chicken
    soup
Pineapple spears or spiced peaches

Heat oven to 350°. Mix all ingredients except pineapple spears in ungreased 2-quart casserole. Cover and bake 1½ hours; stir.

Cover and bake until rice is tender, 15 to 25 minutes longer. Serve with pineapple spears; sprinkle with slivered almonds if desired.

Spicy Chicken and Brown Rice in Peppers: Bake chicken mixture as directed above. Cut 3 green peppers lengthwise into halves; remove seeds and membranes. Cook peppers in boiling water to cover 5 minutes; drain. Fill each pepper half with ¾ cup chicken mixture; sprinkle with slivered almonds if desired.

Turkey with Rice and Pea Pods

2 cups cut-up cooked turkey or chicken
2 cups boiling water
1 can (10¾ ounces) condensed cream of
    mushroom soup
1 package (6¾ ounces) instant long grain and
    wild rice mix (dry)
1 package (6 ounces) frozen Chinese pea pods
1 small onion, chopped

Heat oven to 350°. Mix all ingredients in ungreased 3-quart casserole.

Cover and bake until liquid is absorbed, about 35 minutes. Stir before serving.

Spicy Chicken and Brown Rice

Rice with Beans and Bacon

6 SERVINGS

1 cup uncooked regular rice
1½ cups boiling water
1 tablespoon instant beef bouillon (dry)
1 can (16 ounces) kidney beans, undrained
1 package (10 ounces) frozen baby lima beans
1 medium onion, chopped
6 slices bacon, crisply cooked and crumbled

Heat oven to 350°. Mix all ingredients except bacon in ungreased 2-quart casserole.

Cover and bake until liquid is absorbed, 60 to 65 minutes; stir. Sprinkle with bacon.

Chicken Spaghetti Sauce

6 SERVINGS

1 cup water
1 teaspoon salt
1 teaspoon sugar
1 tablespoon snipped fresh oregano leaves or
    1 teaspoon dried oregano leaves
2 teaspoons snipped fresh basil leaves or
    ¾ teaspoon dried basil leaves
1 teaspoon snipped fresh marjoram leaves or
    ½ teaspoon dried marjoram leaves
½ teaspoon snipped fresh rosemary leaves or
    ¼ teaspoon dried rosemary leaves, if desired
1 large onion, chopped
1 clove garlic, crushed
1 bay leaf
1 can (8 ounces) tomato sauce
1 can (6 ounces) tomato paste
1½ cups cut-up cooked chicken
Hot cooked spaghetti

Heat all ingredients except chicken and spaghetti to boiling in 10-inch skillet; reduce heat. Cover and simmer 30 minutes, stirring occasionally.

Stir in chicken. Cover and simmer 30 minutes, stirring occasionally. Remove bay leaf. Serve sauce over spaghetti. Sprinkle with grated Parmesan cheese if desired.

TO MICROWAVE: Mix ½ cup water and the onion in 2-quart microwavable casserole. Cover tightly and microwave on high (100%) until onion is barely tender, 3 to 4½ minutes.

Stir in seasonings, tomato sauce, tomato paste and ¼ cup water. Cover tightly and microwave 5 minutes; stir in chicken. Cover tightly and microwave on medium-low (30%) until hot, 15 to 18 minutes. Remove bay leaf. Serve as directed above.

Beef Goulash

1½ pounds ground beef
1 medium onion, chopped
1 stalk celery, sliced
1 can (16 ounces) stewed tomatoes
1 tomato can water
1 package (7 ounces) uncooked elbow macaroni
  (2 cups)
1 can (6 ounces) tomato paste
1 tablespoon Worcestershire sauce
1 teaspoon salt
½ teaspoon pepper

Cook and stir ground beef, onion and celery in 4-quart ovenproof Dutch oven until beef is brown; drain. Stir in remaining ingredients.

Cover and bake in 350° oven until liquid is absorbed and goulash is hot, about 40 minutes; stir.

Italian Sausage Goulash: Substitute 1½ pounds bulk Italian sausage for the ground beef. Omit salt and pepper.

TO MICROWAVE: Crumble ground beef into 3-quart microwavable casserole. Cover with waxed paper and microwave on high (100%) 4 minutes; stir. Cover with waxed paper and microwave until very little pink remains, 4 to 5 minutes longer; drain.

Substitute 1½ cups hot water for the 1 tomato can water; stir tomatoes, water and remaining ingredients into beef. Cover tightly and microwave until bubbly around edge, about 10 minutes; stir. Cover tightly and microwave, stirring every 5 minutes, until macaroni is tender and liquid is absorbed, 10 to 15 minutes longer.

Following pages: Baked Spaghetti Sauce (left) and Vegetable Lasagne

Vegetable Lasagne

3 cups chunky-style spaghetti sauce
1 medium zucchini, shredded
6 uncooked lasagne noodles
1 cup ricotta or small curd creamed cottage
　cheese
1/4 cup grated Parmesan cheese
1 tablespoon snipped fresh oregano leaves or
　1 teaspoon dried oregano leaves
2 cups shredded mozzarella cheese (8 ounces)

Mix spaghetti sauce and zucchini. Spread 1 cup mixture in ungreased rectangular baking dish, 11 x 7 x 1½ inches; top with 3 uncooked noodles. Mix ricotta cheese, Parmesan cheese and oregano; spread over noodles in dish. Spread with 1 cup of the sauce mixture.

Top with remaining noodles, sauce mixture and the mozzarella cheese. Bake uncovered in 350° oven until hot and bubbly, about 45 minutes. Let stand 15 minutes before cutting.

Baked Spaghetti Sauce

1 pound ground beef
1 large onion, chopped
1 clove garlic, finely chopped
1 can (10¾ ounces) condensed tomato soup
1 can (8 ounces) mushroom stems and pieces,
　undrained
1 can (8 ounces) tomato sauce
1 can (6 ounces) tomato paste
1/3 cup water
2 teaspoons Italian seasoning
1/2 teaspoon pepper
Hot cooked spaghetti
Grated Parmesan cheese

Cook and stir ground beef, onion and garlic in 4-quart ovenproof Dutch oven until beef is brown; drain. Stir in remaining ingredients except spaghetti and cheese.

Cover and bake in 350° oven 1 hour; stir. Serve over spaghetti; sprinkle with cheese.

TO MICROWAVE: Omit water and decrease Italian seasoning to 1 teaspoon. Crumble ground beef into 3-quart microwavable casserole; add onion and garlic. Cover with waxed paper and microwave on high (100%) 3 minutes; stir. Cover with waxed paper and microwave until beef is no longer pink, 2 to 3 minutes longer; drain.

Stir in remaining ingredients except spaghetti and cheese. Cover tightly and microwave 5 minutes; stir. Cover tightly and microwave on medium (50%) 15 minutes longer. Serve over spaghetti; sprinkle with cheese.

Manicotti

1 jar (32 ounces) chunky-style spaghetti sauce
2 packages (10 ounces each) frozen chopped
   spinach, thawed and well drained
1 container (12 ounces) small curd creamed
   cottage cheese (1½ cups)
⅓ cup grated Parmesan cheese
1 tablespoon snipped fresh oregano leaves or
   1 teaspoon dried oregano leaves
¼ teaspoon pepper
14 uncooked manicotti shells (about 8 ounces)
2 cups shredded mozzarella cheese (8 ounces)

Spread ⅓ of the spaghetti sauce in ungreased rectangular baking dish, 13 x 9 x 2 inches. Mix spinach, cottage cheese, Parmesan cheese, oregano and pepper. Fill uncooked manicotti shells with spinach mixture; arrange on spaghetti sauce in dish.

Pour remaining spaghetti sauce evenly over shells, covering completely; sprinkle with mozzarella cheese. Cover and bake in 350° oven until shells are tender, about 1½ hours.

Cheesy Lasagne

12 SERVINGS

½ cup margarine or butter
½ cup all-purpose flour
½ teaspoon salt
4 cups milk
1 cup shredded Swiss cheese (4 ounces)
1 cup shredded mozzarella cheese (4 ounces)
½ cup grated Parmesan cheese
2 cups small curd creamed cottage cheese
¼ cup snipped parsley
1 tablespoon snipped fresh basil leaves or
   1 teaspoon dried basil leaves
½ teaspoon salt
1 teaspoon snipped fresh oregano leaves or
   ½ teaspoon dried oregano leaves
2 cloves garlic, crushed
12 uncooked lasagne noodles
½ cup grated Parmesan cheese

Heat margarine in 2-quart saucepan over low heat until melted. Stir in flour and ½ teaspoon salt. Cook, stirring constantly, until smooth and bubbly. Remove from heat; stir in milk. Heat to boiling, stirring constantly. Boil and stir 1 minute.

Stir in Swiss cheese, mozzarella cheese and ½ cup Parmesan cheese. Cook and stir over low heat until cheeses are melted. Mix remaining ingredients except noodles and remaining Parmesan cheese.

Spread ¼ of the cheese sauce mixture in ungreased rectangular baking dish, 13 x 9 x 2 inches; top with 4 uncooked noodles. Spread 1 cup of the cottage cheese mixture over noodles; spread with ¼ of the cheese sauce mixture. Repeat with 4 noodles, the remaining cottage cheese mixture, ¼ of the cheese sauce mixture, the remaining noodles and remaining cheese sauce mixture. Sprinkle with ½ cup Parmesan cheese.

Bake uncovered in 350° oven until noodles are done, 35 to 40 minutes. Let stand 10 minutes before cutting.

GRAINS AND PASTA

227

Oven and Grill Dishes

Few cooking methods are as versatile—and often interchangeable —as baking and grilling. Poultry and spareribs in particular adapt beautifully to both techniques and to the microwave, too. Take a look at our recipes for baked ribs. One has microwave instructions and another has a grilled variation.

Grilled Tarragon Chicken Bundles

6 SERVINGS

6 boneless skinless chicken breast halves (about
   1 1/2 pounds)
6 medium carrots, cut lengthwise into quarters,
   then into 3-inch pieces
4 ounces mushrooms
6 small zucchini, cut lengthwise into quarters,
   then into 3-inch pieces
1/2 cup margarine or butter, melted
1 tablespoon snipped fresh tarragon leaves or
   1 teaspoon dried tarragon leaves
1 teaspoon salt
1/4 teaspoon pepper

Place chicken breast half on each of 6 pieces heavy-duty aluminum foil, 18 x 14 inches; top with vegetables. Drizzle with margarine; sprinkle with tarragon, salt and pepper. Wrap securely in foil.

Grill bundles 5 to 6 inches from hot coals until chicken is done and vegetables are tender, 45 to 60 minutes.

TO BAKE: Bake bundles in shallow pan in 350° oven until chicken is done and vegetables are tender, 50 to 60 minutes.

Grilled Tarragon Chicken Bundle

Mexican-style Chicken

3 tablespoons vegetable oil
2½- to 3½-pound broiler-fryer chicken, cut up
½ cup all-purpose flour
2½ cups boiling water
1½ teaspoons salt
1½ to 2 teaspoons chili powder
⅛ teaspoon pepper
Dash of ground red pepper
1 can (28 ounces) whole tomatoes, undrained
1 medium onion, chopped
2 chicken bouillon cubes or 2 teaspoons instant
    chicken bouillon (dry)
1 clove garlic, finely chopped
1 cup uncooked regular rice
1 can (8 ounces) whole kernel corn, undrained
1 can (8 ounces) kidney beans, undrained

Heat oil in 4-quart ovenproof Dutch oven or 10-inch ovenproof skillet. Coat chicken with flour. Cook in hot oil over medium heat until brown, 15 to 20 minutes; drain.

Mix remaining ingredients except rice, corn and beans; pour over chicken. Cover and bake in 350° oven 30 minutes. Stir in rice, corn and beans. Cover and bake until chicken is done and rice is tender, 30 to 40 minutes. Serve with tortilla chips if desired.

TO MICROWAVE: Omit oil and flour. Decrease water to 1 cup. Arrange chicken, skin sides up and thickest parts to outside edge, in 3-quart microwavable casserole. Cover tightly and microwave on high (100%) 10 minutes; rotate casserole ½ turn. Microwave 5 minutes longer; drain.

Mix remaining ingredients except corn and beans; break up tomatoes. Stir into chicken. Cover tightly and microwave, stirring every 8 minutes, until thickest pieces of chicken are done and rice is tender, 25 to 30 minutes. Drain corn and beans; stir into chicken mixture. Cover tightly and microwave until corn and beans are hot, 4 to 6 minutes.

Grilled Lemon Chicken

2½- to 3-pound broiler-fryer chicken, cut up
½ cup dry white wine
¼ cup lemon juice
2 tablespoons vegetable oil
1 teaspoon paprika
1 lemon, thinly sliced
1 clove garlic, crushed
1 lemon, thinly sliced
Paprika

Place chicken in glass or plastic bowl. Mix remaining ingredients except 1 lemon and paprika; pour over chicken. Cover and refrigerate at least 3 hours.

Remove chicken and lemon slices. Discard lemon slices; reserve marinade. Cover and grill chicken, bone sides down, 5 to 6 inches from medium coals 15 to 20 minutes; turn chicken. Cover and grill, turning and brushing 2 or 3 times with marinade, until chicken is done, 20 to 40 minutes longer.

Roll edges of remaining lemon slices in paprika; arrange around chicken. Garnish with celery leaves if desired.

TO MICROWAVE: Prepare marinade and marinate chicken in 2-quart microwavable casserole as directed above. Remove chicken and lemon slices from marinade. Discard slices; reserve marinade.

Arrange chicken, skin sides up and thickest parts to outside edge, in casserole. Cover tightly and microwave on high (100%) 12 minutes.

Place chicken, bone sides down and 5 to 6 inches from medium coals, on grill. Cover and grill, turning and brushing 2 or 3 times with marinade, until done, 15 to 20 minutes.

Baked Barbecued Chicken

2¹/₂- to 3-pound broiler-fryer chicken, cut up
³/₄ cup chili sauce
2 tablespoons honey
2 tablespoons soy sauce
1 teaspoon dry mustard
¹/₂ teaspoon prepared horseradish
¹/₂ teaspoon red pepper sauce

Place chicken, skin sides up, in ungreased rectangular pan, 13 x 9 x 2 inches. Mix remaining ingredients; pour over chicken. Cover and bake in 375° oven 30 minutes. Spoon sauce over chicken; bake uncovered until thickest pieces are done, about 30 minutes longer.

TO MICROWAVE: Arrange chicken, skin sides up and thickest parts to outside edges, in rectangular microwavable dish, 12 x 7¹/₂ x 2 inches. Mix remaining ingredients; pour over chicken. Cover with waxed paper and microwave on high (100%) 10 minutes. Spoon sauce over chicken; rotate dish ¹/₂ turn. Cover with waxed paper and microwave until thickest pieces are done, 6 to 10 minutes longer.

Herbed Chicken

2 tablespoons margarine or butter
2 tablespoons olive or vegetable oil
¹/₄ cup finely chopped onion
¹/₄ cup lemon juice
2 tablespoons Worcestershire sauce
1¹/₂ teaspoons snipped fresh basil leaves or
    ¹/₂ teaspoon dried basil leaves
³/₄ teaspoon snipped fresh marjoram leaves or ¹/₄
    teaspoon dried marjoram leaves
³/₄ teaspoon snipped fresh oregano leaves or
    ¹/₄ teaspoon dried oregano leaves
2 large cloves garlic, finely chopped
2¹/₂- to 3-pound broiler-fryer chicken, cut up

Heat margarine and oil in rectangular pan, 13 x 9 x 2 inches, in 375° oven until margarine is melted. Stir in remaining ingredients except chicken. Place chicken, skin sides up, in pan, turning to coat with herb mixture. Bake uncovered 30 minutes. Turn chicken; bake uncovered until thickest pieces are done, about 30 minutes longer.

TO MICROWAVE: Place margarine and oil in rectangular microwavable dish, 12 x 7¹/₂ x 2 inches. Microwave uncovered on high (100%) until margarine is melted, 45 to 60 seconds. Stir in remaining ingredients except chicken. Place chicken in dish, turning to coat with herb mixture. Arrange chicken, skin sides up and thickest parts to outside edges, in dish. Cover with waxed paper and microwave on high (100%) 10 minutes; rotate dish ¹/₂ turn. Microwave until thickest pieces are done, 6 to 10 minutes.

Herbed Rock Cornish Hens

3 Rock Cornish hens (about 1 1/4 pounds each),
   thawed
Salt and pepper
1/4 cup margarine or butter, melted
1 1/2 teaspoons snipped fresh thyme leaves or
   1/2 teaspoon dried thyme leaves
1 1/2 teaspoons snipped fresh marjoram leaves or
   1/2 teaspoon dried marjoram leaves
1/4 teaspoon paprika

Rub cavities of hens with salt and pepper. Place hens, breast sides up, on rack in shallow roasting pan. Mix remaining ingredients; brush hens with some of the margarine mixture.

Roast uncovered in 350° oven, brushing with margarine mixture 5 or 6 times, until done, about 1 1/4 hours. Cut each hen along backbone from tail to neck into halves with kitchen scissors.

Tarragon Rock Cornish Hens: Omit thyme and marjoram; mix margarine and 1 tablespoon snipped fresh tarragon leaves or 1 teaspoon dried tarragon leaves, 2 tablespoons lemon juice and 1 teaspoon snipped chives.

TO GRILL: Prepare hens and margarine mixture as directed above. Insert spit rod through cavities of hens from breast ends toward tails; hold firmly in place with adjustable holding forks. Brush hens with margarine mixture. Arrange medium-hot coals at back of firebox; place foil drip pan under spit area. Cook hens on rotisserie, brushing frequently with margarine mixture, until done, 1 to 1 1/2 hours.

Gingered Chicken with Pea Pods

2½- to 3-pound whole broiler-fryer chicken
¼ cup margarine or butter, melted
¼ teaspoon paprika
¼ teaspoon ground ginger
8 ounces fresh Chinese pea pods or 2 packages
   (6 ounces each) frozen Chinese pea pods
1 medium onion, cut into thin wedges
½ teaspoon ground turmeric
¼ teaspoon ground ginger
2 tablespoons margarine or butter
8 ounces medium mushrooms
1 teaspoon salt
2 teaspoons lemon juice
8 cherry tomatoes, cut into halves

Fold wings of chicken across back with tips touching. Tie drumsticks to tail. Place chicken, breast side up, on rack in shallow roasting pan. Mix ¼ cup margarine, the paprika and ¼ teaspoon ginger; generously brush over chicken. Roast uncovered in 375° oven, brushing with margarine mixture 2 or 3 times, until thickcst parts are done, about 1¼ hours.

About 15 minutes before chicken is done, rinse frozen pea pods with cold water to separate; drain. Cook and stir onion, turmeric and ¼ teaspoon ginger in 2 tablespoons margarine in 10-inch skillet over medium heat until onion is almost tender, about 3 minutes.

Stir in pea pods, mushrooms, salt and lemon juice. Cook uncovered, stirring occasionally, until pea pods are hot, about 5 minutes. Stir in tomatoes; heat just until hot. Serve vegetables with chicken.

TO MICROWAVE: Prepare chicken for roasting as directed above. Place chicken, breast side down, in square microwavable dish, 8 x 8 x 2 inches. Microwave uncovered on high (100%) 12 minutes.

Turn chicken, breast side up. Decrease ¼ cup melted margarine to 2 tablespoons. Mix melted margarine, paprika and ¼ teaspoon ginger; brush over chicken. Microwave uncovered until drumstick meat feels very soft when pressed between fingers, 10 to 14 minutes. Cover and keep warm.

Rinse frozen pea pods as directed above. Mix onion, turmeric, ¼ teaspoon ginger and 2 tablespoons margarine in 1½-quart microwavable casserole. Cover tightly and microwave on high (100%) until onion is tender, 2 to 4 minutes; add pea pods, mushrooms, salt and lemon juice. Cover tightly and microwave until pea pods are tender, 4 to 7 minutes. Stir in tomatoes; let stand uncovered 3 minutes. Serve vegetables with chicken.

Gingered Chicken with Pea Pods

Turkey Divan

1/4 cup margarine or butter
1/4 cup all-purpose flour
1/8 teaspoon ground nutmeg
1 1/2 cups chicken broth
1/2 cup grated Parmesan cheese
2 tablespoons dry white wine
1/2 cup chilled whipping cream
1 1/2 pounds fresh broccoli or 2 packages
    (10 ounces each) frozen broccoli spears,
    cooked and drained
5 large slices cooked turkey breast (about
    3/4 pound)
1/2 cup grated Parmesan cheese

Heat margarine in 1-quart saucepan over low heat until melted. Stir in flour and nutmeg. Cook, stirring constantly, until smooth and bubbly. Remove from heat; stir in broth.

Heat to boiling, stirring constantly. Boil and stir 1 minute. Remove from heat; stir in 1/2 cup cheese and the wine. Beat whipping cream in chilled medium bowl until stiff. Fold cheese sauce into whipped cream.

Arrange hot broccoli in ungreased rectangular baking dish, 12 x 7 1/2 x 2 inches; top with turkey. Pour cheese sauce over turkey; sprinkle with 1/2 cup cheese. Set oven control to broil. Broil with top 3 to 5 inches from heat until cheese is bubbly and light brown.

TO MICROWAVE: Microwave margarine in 1-quart microwavable measure uncovered on high (100%) until melted, 1 to 2 minutes. Decrease chicken broth to 1 cup. Stir flour, nutmeg and broth into margarine. Microwave uncovered, stirring every minute, until sauce is thickened, 4 to 5 minutes.

Continue as directed above except use rectangular microwavable dish, 12 x 7 1/2 x 2 inches. Cover tightly and microwave on high (100%) until hot, 5 to 7 minutes.

Fish with Zucchini and Green Peppers

4 SERVINGS

1 pound fish fillets
½ teaspoon salt
⅛ teaspoon pepper
2 tablespoons margarine or butter, melted
1 tablespoon lemon juice
1 medium zucchini, cut into ¼-inch slices
1 small green pepper, cut into ¼-inch strips
1 small red onion, sliced
2 tablespoons margarine or butter

If fish fillets are large, cut into 4 serving pieces. Arrange fish in ungreased rectangular baking dish, 12 x 7½ x 2 inches, or square baking dish, 8 x 8 x 2 inches; sprinkle with salt and pepper. Mix 2 tablespoons margarine and the lemon juice; pour over fish. Bake uncovered in 350° oven until fish flakes easily with fork, 20 to 25 minutes.

Cook zucchini, green pepper and onion in 2 tablespoons margarine over medium heat, stirring occasionally, until crisp-tender, 5 to 7 minutes. Serve vegetables over fish.

TO MICROWAVE: Decrease melted margarine to 1 tablespoon; omit 2 tablespoons margarine. If fish fillets are large, cut into 4 serving pieces; pat dry. Arrange fish, with thickest parts to outside edges, in square microwavable dish, 8 x 8 x 2 inches; sprinkle with salt and pepper.

Top with vegetables. Mix melted margarine and lemon juice; pour over vegetables. Cover with vented plastic wrap and microwave on high (100%) 4 minutes; rotate dish ½ turn. Microwave until fish flakes easily with fork and vegetables are crisp-tender, 4 to 5 minutes longer.

Fish Baked in Lettuce Packets

6 large or 12 small lettuce leaves*
1 medium carrot, shredded
1 small zucchini, shredded
1½ pounds fish fillets, cut into 6 serving
   pieces**
1 tablespoon snipped fresh marjoram leaves or
   1 teaspoon dried marjoram leaves
Salt and pepper to taste
Margarine or butter

Heat oven to 400°. Place a few lettuce leaves at a time in hot water. Let stand until wilted, 1 to 2 minutes; drain. Mound a portion of carrot and zucchini near stem end of each lettuce leaf. Place 1 piece fish on vegetables. Sprinkle with marjoram, salt and pepper; dot with margarine.

Fold lettuce leaf over fish; place seam sides down in ungreased rectangular baking dish, 13 x 9 x 2 inches. (Vegetables should be on top of fish.) Cover and bake until fish is done, 25 to 30 minutes.

✽ 6 pieces aluminum foil, about 12 x 8 inches each, can be substituted for the 6 large lettuce leaves. Place 1 piece fish on center of each piece foil; mound a portion of carrot and zucchini on each piece fish. Fold foil over fish and vegetables and seal securely. Place seam side up in baking dish. Do not cover.

✽✽ If using 12 small lettuce leaves, cut fish into 12 pieces.

TO MICROWAVE: Prepare lettuce and wrap vegetables and fish as directed above (do not use aluminum foil substitution). Place seam sides down in rectangular microwavable dish, 12 x 7½ x 2 inches. Cover with vented plastic wrap and microwave on high (100%) 4 minutes; rotate dish ½ turn. Microwave until fish is done, 5 to 6 minutes longer.

Fish Baked in Lettuce Packet

OVEN AND GRILL DISHES

Herbed Fish Steaks

2 medium carrots, cut into thin strips
1 medium leek, cut into thin strips
1 medium zucchini, cut into thin strips
1 medium stalk celery, cut into thin strips
3 fish steaks, each 1 inch thick (about 2 pounds)
1/4 cup margarine or butter, melted
1 1/2 teaspoons snipped fresh marjoram leaves or
    1/2 teaspoon dried marjoram leaves
1 1/2 teaspoons snipped fresh rosemary leaves or
    1/2 teaspoon dried rosemary leaves, crushed
1 teaspoon salt
6 thin lemon slices

Heat oven to 400°. Mix vegetables and arrange in ungreased rectangular baking dish, 12 x 7½ x 2 inches. Cut each fish steak into halves; arrange on vegetables. Drizzle with margarine; sprinkle with herbs and salt. Place lemon slice on each piece fish. Cover and bake until fish flakes easily with fork, 35 to 40 minutes.

TO MICROWAVE: Coarsely shred carrots and decrease margarine to 2 tablespoons. Arrange vegetables and fish as directed above in rectangular microwavable dish, 12 x 7½ x 2 inches. Drizzle with margarine; sprinkle with herbs and salt. Place lemon slice on each piece fish. Cover with vented plastic wrap and microwave on high (100%) 5 minutes; rotate dish ½ turn. Microwave until fish flakes easily with fork, 6 to 8 minutes longer.

Company Pot Roast

3- to 4-pound beef rolled rump roast*
3 tablespoons vegetable oil
¾ cup dairy sour cream
¾ cup dry red wine
½ teaspoon salt
½ teaspoon pepper
½ teaspoon dried thyme leaves
2 cloves garlic, finely chopped
2 medium carrots, cut crosswise into 1-inch
    pieces
2 medium onions, sliced and separated into rings
½ cup water
2 tablespoons all-purpose flour
1 tablespoon lemon juice

Cook beef roast in oil in 4-quart ovenproof Dutch oven until brown; remove beef. Mix remaining ingredients except water, flour and lemon juice in Dutch oven.

Return beef to Dutch oven. Cover and bake in 325° oven until beef is tender, about 3½ hours. Remove beef to heated platter; keep warm while preparing gravy.

Skim fat from liquid. Shake water and flour in tightly covered container; gradually stir into liquid. Heat to boiling, stirring constantly. Boil and stir 1 minute. Stir in lemon juice; cook 1 minute. Slice beef thinly; serve with gravy.

✳ Beef bottom round or boneless chuck eye roast can be substituted for the rolled rump roast.

TO MICROWAVE: Omit oil; increase flour to 3 tablespoons. Place 3-pound beef roast in 3-quart microwavable casserole. Cover tightly and microwave on high (100%) 12 minutes; drain.

Mix remaining ingredients except water, flour and lemon juice; add to casserole, spooning some of mixture over beef. Cover tightly and microwave 10 minutes; rotate casserole ½ turn. Microwave on medium-low (30%) 1 hour; turn beef over. Cover tightly and microwave until beef is tender, 45 minutes to 1 hour longer. Remove beef and vegetables to heated platter; keep warm.

Mix water and flour and stir into liquid as directed above. Microwave uncovered on high (100%) 2 minutes; stir in lemon juice. Microwave uncovered until thickened, 1 to 2 minutes longer. Serve beef as directed above.

Following pages: Company Pot Roast

Mexican Grilled Steak

2 high-quality beef flank steaks (1 to 1½ pounds
    each)
Juice of 2 limes (about ½ cup)
4 cloves garlic, crushed
⅓ cup snipped fresh oregano leaves or
    2 tablespoons dried oregano leaves
2 tablespoons olive or vegetable oil
2 teaspoons salt
½ teaspoon pepper

Place beef steaks in shallow glass or plastic dish. Mix remaining ingredients; pour over beef. Cover and refrigerate at least 8 hours but no longer than 24 hours, turning beef occasionally.

Cover and grill beef 4 to 5 inches from medium coals, turning once, until desired doneness, 10 to 15 minutes for medium. Cut beef across grain at slanted angle into thin slices. Serve with tortillas and guacamole if desired.

TO BROIL: Marinate beef steaks as directed above. Set oven control to broil. Place beef on rack in broiler pan. Broil with tops 2 to 3 inches from heat until brown, about 5 minutes. Turn beef; broil 5 minutes longer. Cut and serve as directed above.

Mexican Grilled Steak

Short Ribs and Sauerkraut

5 SERVINGS

2 pounds beef short ribs, cut into serving pieces
1/2 cup raisins
1/3 cup packed brown sugar
1 cup apple juice
2 medium tart cooking apples, sliced
2 cans (16 ounces each) sauerkraut, drained

Arrange beef ribs in 4-quart ovenproof Dutch oven. Mix remaining ingredients; pour over beef.

Cover and bake in 325° oven until beef is tender, about 2½ hours.

Meat Loaves Wrapped in Bacon

6 SERVINGS

1½ pounds ground beef
1 small onion, chopped
1 egg
1 cup shredded Cheddar cheese (4 ounces)
1/4 cup dry bread crumbs
1/4 cup chopped green pepper
1/2 cup water
1/4 cup lemon juice
1 teaspoon salt
1/2 teaspoon instant beef bouillon (dry)
6 slices thin-sliced bacon, cut into halves

Heat oven to 350°. Mix all ingredients except bacon. Shape mixture into 6 loaves.

Crisscross 2 half-slices bacon on each loaf, tucking ends under loaf. Place loaves on rack in shallow baking pan. Bake uncovered 50 minutes.

TO MICROWAVE: Shape 6 loaves as directed above. Arrange loaves on microwavable rack in microwavable dish or in circle on 12-inch microwavable plate. Cover with waxed paper and microwave on high (100%) 5 minutes; rotate dish ½ turn. Microwave until loaves are almost done, 7 to 10 minutes longer. Let stand covered 5 minutes.

Place bacon on 10- or 12-inch microwavable plate lined with microwavable paper towel. Cover with paper towel and microwave on high (100%) until crisp, 4 to 7 minutes. Crisscross 2 half-slices bacon on each loaf.

Short Ribs and Sauerkraut

Veal Shanks with Olives

4 SERVINGS

4 pounds veal shanks, cut into 2½-inch pieces
3 tablespoons quick-cooking tapioca
1 teaspoon snipped fresh basil leaves or
  ½ teaspoon dried basil leaves
¼ teaspoon pepper
1 clove garlic, crushed
Grated peel of 1 lemon (about 1 tablespoon)
1 can (8 ounces) sliced water chestnuts, drained
1 jar (2½ ounces) small pitted Spanish olives,
  drained
⅓ cup dry white wine or water
1 can (10½ ounces) condensed beef broth

Trim excess fat from veal shanks if necessary. Place veal in 4-quart ovenproof Dutch oven. Sprinkle with tapioca, basil, pepper, garlic and lemon peel. Add water chestnuts and olives; pour wine and broth over top.

Cover and bake in 325° oven until veal shanks are tender, about 2 hours. Serve with hot cooked noodles if desired.

Beef Shanks with Olives: Substitute beef shanks for the veal shanks.

Veal Shank with Olives

Veal Chops with Mustard

4 veal rib or loin chops, each ¾ inch thick*
1 to 2 tablespoons prepared mustard
½ teaspoon pepper
6 slices bacon, cut into ½-inch pieces
¾ cup whipping cream
2 tablespoons capers

Brush both sides of each veal chop lightly with mustard; sprinkle with pepper. Place in ungreased square pan, 9 x 9 x 2 inches. Sprinkle bacon over and around veal. Bake uncovered in 350° oven until veal is tender, about 1 hour.

Remove veal to warm platter. Skim fat from drippings, reserving ¼ cup drippings and the bacon in pan. Stir whipping cream into pan. Heat to boiling, stirring constantly; reduce heat slightly. Cook uncovered, stirring frequently, until thickened, about 8 minutes. Stir in capers; pour sauce over veal.

✱ 2 veal sirloin chops, cut into halves, can be substituted for the veal rib or loin chops.

TO MICROWAVE: Place bacon in 2-cup microwavable measure. Cover loosely and microwave on high (100%) until partially cooked but not crisp, 1½ to 3 minutes.

Brush both sides of each veal chop lightly with mustard; sprinkle with pepper. Arrange in square microwavable dish, 9 x 9 x 2 inches. Sprinkle bacon over and around veal. Cover tightly and microwave on medium (50%) 10 minutes; turn chops over and rotate dish ½ turn. Cover tightly and microwave until veal is done, 10 to 13 minutes longer.

Remove veal to warm platter. Drain drippings, reserving 1 tablespoon drippings and bacon in dish. Stir whipping cream into dish. Microwave uncovered on high (100%), stirring every minute, until sauce is consistency of thin white sauce, 2½ to 4 minutes. Stir in capers; pour sauce over veal.

Baked Spareribs with Spicy Barbecue Sauce

6 SERVINGS

4½-pound rack fresh pork loin back ribs, cut
  into serving pieces
Spicy Barbecue Sauce (below)

Place pork ribs, meaty sides up, on rack in shallow roasting pan. Roast uncovered in 325° oven 1½ hours.

Brush with Spicy Barbecue Sauce. Roast, turning and brushing frequently with sauce, until done, about 45 minutes longer. Serve with remaining sauce.

SPICY BARBECUE SAUCE

⅓ cup margarine or butter
2 tablespoons vinegar
2 tablespoons water
1 teaspoon sugar
½ teaspoon garlic powder
½ teaspoon onion powder
½ teaspoon pepper
Dash of ground red pepper

Heat all ingredients, stirring frequently, until margarine is melted.

TO GRILL: Place pork ribs in 4-quart Dutch oven; add 3 cups water. Heat to boiling; reduce heat. Cover and simmer 5 minutes; drain. Cover and grill pork 5 to 6 inches from medium coals, brushing with Spicy Barbecue Sauce every 3 minutes, until done and meat begins to pull away from bones (170°), 15 to 20 minutes.

Following pages: Baked Spareribs with Spicy Barbecue Sauce

Barbecued Country-style Spareribs

1 teaspoon garlic powder
1 teaspoon onion powder
1 teaspoon salt
4½ pounds fresh pork country-style ribs, cut into serving pieces
⅔ cup catsup
1 tablespoon dry mustard
2 tablespoons Worcestershire sauce
1 teaspoon chili powder
½ teaspoon liquid smoke
¼ teaspoon red pepper sauce

Mix garlic powder, onion powder and salt; rub on pork ribs. Place meaty sides up on rack in shallow roasting pan. Roast uncovered in 325° oven 1 hour.

Mix remaining ingredients. Cover and grill pork 5 to 6 inches from medium coals, turning and brushing 2 or 3 times with catsup mixture, until done and meat begins to pull away from bones (170°), 20 to 30 minutes. Pour remaining catsup mixture over pork before serving.

TO MICROWAVE: Mix garlic powder, onion powder and salt; rub on pork ribs. Arrange meaty sides up in 3-quart microwavable casserole. Cover loosely and microwave on medium-high (70%), rearranging pork every 10 minutes, until almost no pink remains, 26 to 32 minutes. Prepare catsup mixture and grill pork as directed above.

Pork Sausage and Bean Casserole

1 pound bulk pork sausage
2 medium stalks celery, sliced
1 medium onion, chopped
1 large clove garlic, crushed
2 cans (21 ounces each) baked beans in tomato
  sauce
1 can (16 ounces) lima beans, drained
1 can (15½ ounces) kidney beans, drained
1 can (8 ounces) tomato sauce
1 tablespoon dry mustard
2 tablespoons honey
1 tablespoon vinegar
1 teaspoon salt
¼ teaspoon red pepper sauce

Cook and stir sausage, celery, onion and garlic until sausage is brown, about 10 minutes; drain. Mix sausage mixture and remaining ingredients in ungreased 3-quart casserole.

Bake uncovered in 400° oven, stirring once, until hot and bubbly, about 45 minutes.

TO MICROWAVE: Place sausage, celery, onion and garlic in 3-quart microwavable casserole. Cover tightly and microwave on high (100%) 4 minutes; stir. Cover tightly and microwave until sausage is no longer pink, 2 to 5 minutes longer; drain.

Mix sausage mixture and remaining ingredients in same casserole. Cover tightly and microwave 10 minutes; stir. Cover tightly and microwave on medium (50%) to blend flavors, 15 minutes.

Ham Steak with Mustard Fruit

1 fully cooked smoked ham slice, about 1 inch
   thick (about 2 pounds)
1 can (30 ounces) apricot halves, drained
1 can (15¼ ounces) pineapple chunks, drained
¼ cup margarine or butter, melted
2 tablespoons prepared mustard
2 tablespoons honey
1 teaspoon prepared horseradish
1 medium clove garlic, crushed

Slash outer edge of fat on ham diagonally at 1-inch intervals to prevent curling. Place ham in ungreased rectangular baking dish, 12 x 7½ x 2 inches. Arrange fruit on ham.

Mix remaining ingredients; pour over fruit and ham. Bake uncovered in 350° oven until ham is hot, about 40 minutes. Serve with buttered sugar snap peas or Chinese pea pods if desired

TO MICROWAVE: Prepare ham as directed above. Place ham in rectangular microwavable dish, 12 x 7½ x 2 inches. Cover with waxed paper and microwave on medium-high (70%) 8 minutes. Turn ham; arrange fruit on ham. Mix remaining ingredients; pour over fruit and ham. Cover with waxed paper and microwave 5 minutes; rotate dish ½ turn. Microwave until ham is hot, 5 to 7 minutes longer. Serve as directed above if desired.

Baked Sausage and Wild Rice

2 pounds bulk pork sausage
1 medium onion, chopped
2 cups cooked wild rice
2 cups cooked regular rice
½ cup shredded Swiss cheese (2 ounces)
1½ cups milk
1 small green pepper, chopped
1 can (10¾ ounces) condensed cream of chicken
   soup
1 can (4 ounces) mushroom stems and pieces,
   drained
1 jar (2 ounces) diced pimientos, drained
¼ cup toasted sliced almonds

Cook and stir sausage and onion in 4-quart Dutch oven until sausage is brown; drain. Stir in remaining ingredients except almonds. Pour into ungreased 3-quart casserole.

Cover and bake in 350° oven until center is bubbly, 45 to 50 minutes. Stir and sprinkle with almonds. Garnish with parsley if desired.

Ham Steak with Mustard Fruit

Calzone and Pizza

These mouth-watering but simple pizza variations aren't just for kids. Pick a crust (thin, deep-dish or Chicago-style deep-dish), spread it with zesty tomato sauce, add your favorite toppings and sprinkle generously with mozzarella cheese. You're guaranteed to have a table full of grinning faces.

Italian Sausage Calzone

4 SERVINGS

½ pound bulk Italian sausage
¼ cup chopped onion
⅓ cup pizza sauce
1 can (2 ounces) mushroom stems and pieces, drained
2 cups baking mix
⅓ cup hot water
1 tablespoon vegetable oil
1 cup shredded mozzarella cheese (4 ounces)
¼ cup grated Parmesan cheese
1 egg white

Heat oven to 450°. Cook and stir sausage until brown; drain. Stir in onion, pizza sauce and mushrooms; reserve.

Mix baking mix, hot water and oil until dough forms. Roll into 12-inch circle on cloth-covered surface dusted with baking mix. Place on ungreased cookie sheet.

Top half of the circle with mozzarella cheese, sausage mixture and Parmesan cheese to within 1 inch of edge. Fold dough over filling; press edge with fork to seal. Brush with egg white. Bake until golden brown, 15 to 20 minutes. Cool 5 minutes; cut into wedges.

Italian Sausage Calzone

Chicken and Spinach Calzone

Calzone Dough (below)
1½ cups shredded Swiss cheese (6 ounces)
1 cup cut-up cooked chicken
¼ cup grated Parmesan cheese
2 teaspoons snipped fresh thyme leaves or
  ½ teaspoon dried thyme leaves
1 clove garlic, finely chopped
1 small onion, chopped
1 can (10¾ ounces) condensed cream of chicken
  soup
1 package (10 ounces) frozen chopped spinach,
  thawed and squeezed dry
1 egg, beaten

Heat oven to 375°. Prepare Calzone Dough. Divide into 6 equal pieces. Pat each into 7-inch circle on lightly floured surface, turning dough over occasionally to coat with flour. Mix remaining ingredients except egg.

Top half of each circle with ⅔ cup chicken mixture to within 1 inch of edge. Fold dough over filling; fold edge up and pinch securely to seal. Place on greased cookie sheet; brush with egg. Bake until golden brown, 25 to 30 minutes.

CALZONE DOUGH

1 package active dry yeast
1 cup warm water (105° to 115°)
1 tablespoon sugar
2 tablespoons vegetable oil
1 teaspoon salt
2¾ to 3¼ cups all-purpose flour

Dissolve yeast in warm water in large bowl. Stir in sugar, oil, salt and 1 cup of the flour. Beat until smooth. Mix in enough remaining flour to make dough easy to handle.

Turn dough onto lightly floured surface; knead until smooth and elastic, about 5 minutes. Cover with bowl and let rest 5 minutes.

Sourdough Corned Beef Calzone

Sourdough Calzone Dough (below)
½ pound thinly sliced cooked corned beef, shredded*
1 can (8 ounces) sauerkraut, drained and pressed dry
1 package (6 ounces) shredded Swiss cheese (about 1¼ cups)
½ cup Thousand Island dressing
1 egg, beaten

Heat oven to 375° Prepare Sourdough Calzone Dough. Divide into 6 equal pieces. Roll each into 7-inch circle on lightly floured surface, turning dough over occasionally to coat with flour. Mix remaining ingredients except egg.

Top half of each circle with ⅔ cup corned beef mixture to within 1 inch of edge. Fold dough over filling; fold edge up and pinch securely to seal. Place on greased cookie sheet; brush with egg. Sprinkle with caraway seed if desired. Bake until golden brown, 30 to 35 minutes.

✱ 1 can (12 ounces) corned beef, crumbled, can be substituted for the sliced corned beef.

SOURDOUGH CALZONE DOUGH

1 package active dry yeast
¼ cup warm water (105° to 115°)
2 tablespoons vegetable oil
1 teaspoon sugar
1 teaspoon salt
1 container (6 ounces) plain yogurt (about ⅔ cup)
2½ to 3 cups all-purpose flour

Dissolve yeast in warm water in large bowl. Stir in oil, sugar, salt, yogurt and 1 cup of the flour. Beat until smooth. Mix in enough remaining flour to make dough easy to handle.

Turn dough onto lightly floured surface; knead until smooth and elastic, about 5 minutes. Cover with bowl and let rest 5 minutes.

Whole Wheat Vegetable Calzone

Whole Wheat Calzone Dough (below)
1 package (10 ounces) frozen chopped broccoli
1/3 cup creamy Italian dressing
1/2 teaspoon salt
1 package (3 ounces) cream cheese, softened
1 cup sliced mushrooms or 1 jar (4.5 ounces)
   sliced mushrooms, drained
2 carrots, shredded
1 medium tomato, chopped
1/2 small green pepper, chopped
1 egg, beaten

Heat oven to 375°. Prepare Whole Wheat Calzone Dough. Divide into 6 equal pieces. Pat each into 7-inch circle on lightly floured surface, turning dough over occasionally to coat with flour.

Rinse frozen broccoli in cold water to separate; drain. Mix dressing, salt and cream cheese until well blended (mixture will appear curdled). Stir in broccoli and remaining vegetables.

Top half of each circle with 2/3 cup vegetable mixture to within 1 inch of edge. Fold dough over filling; fold edge up and pinch securely to seal. Place on greased cookie sheet; brush with egg. Sprinkle with coarse salt if desired. Bake until golden brown, 25 to 30 minutes.

WHOLE WHEAT CALZONE DOUGH

1 package active dry yeast
1 cup warm water (105° to 115°)
1 tablespoon sugar
2 tablespoons vegetable oil
1 teaspoon salt
2 1/2 to 3 cups whole wheat flour

Dissolve yeast in warm water in large bowl. Stir in sugar, oil, salt and 1 cup of the flour. Beat until smooth. Mix in enough remaining flour to make dough easy to handle.

Turn dough onto lightly floured surface; knead until smooth and elastic, about 5 minutes. Cover with bowl and let rest 5 minutes.

Whole Wheat Vegetable Calzone

Thin-crust Pizza

Thin Crust (below)
Sauce (below)
Meat Toppings (below)
Vegetable Toppings (below)
1½ cups shredded mozzarella cheese (6 ounces)

Place oven rack in lowest position of oven. Heat oven to 450°. Prepare Thin Crust; spread with Sauce. Top with one of the Meat Toppings and desired Vegetable Toppings. Sprinkle with mozzarella cheese. Bake on lowest oven rack until crust is brown and cheese is melted and bubbly, 12 to 15 minutes.

THIN CRUST

1½ cups baking mix
⅓ cup very hot water

Mix baking mix and water; beat vigorously 20 strokes. Turn dough onto surface generously dusted with baking mix. Knead until smooth and no longer sticky, about 60 times.

Press dough into 13-inch circle on greased cookie sheet or press in greased 12-inch pizza pan with hands dipped in baking mix. Pinch edge, forming ½-inch rim.

SAUCE

1 can (8 ounces) tomato sauce
1 teaspoon Italian seasoning
⅛ teaspoon garlic powder.

Mix all ingredients.

MEAT TOPPINGS

½ to 1 pound ground beef, cooked and drained
½ to 1 pound bulk Italian sausage, cooked and drained
1 package (3½ ounces) sliced pepperoni
1 package (6 ounces) sliced Canadian-style bacon

VEGETABLE TOPPINGS

Sliced mushrooms
Chopped green pepper
Sliced green onions or chopped onion
Sliced ripe olives

Chicago-style Deep-dish Pizza

Chicago-style Deep-dish Crust (below)
4 cups shredded mozzarella cheese (16 ounces)
Meat Toppings (below)
Vegetable Toppings (below)
1 can (28 ounces) Italian plum tomatoes, chopped and well drained
1 tablespoon snipped fresh oregano leaves or 1 to 2 teaspoons dried oregano leaves or Italian herb seasoning
¼ to ½ cup grated Parmesan cheese

Place oven rack in lowest position of oven. Heat oven to 425°. Prepare Deep-dish Crust; sprinkle with mozzarella cheese. Top with one of the Meat Toppings, desired Vegetable Toppings and tomatoes; sprinkle with oregano and Parmesan cheese. Bake on lowest oven rack until crust is brown and cheese is melted and bubbly, 20 to 25 minutes.

CHICAGO-STYLE DEEP-DISH CRUST

1 package active dry yeast
¾ cup warm water (105° to 115°)
3 cups baking mix
2 tablespoons olive oil

Dissolve yeast in warm water in large bowl. Stir in baking mix and olive oil; beat vigorously 20 strokes. Turn dough onto surface generously dusted with baking mix. Knead dough until smooth and no longer sticky, about 60 times. Let rest 5 minutes.

Press in bottom and up sides of jelly roll pan, 15½ x 10½ x 1 inch, greased with olive oil if desired. Or divide dough into halves and press in bottom and up sides of 2 round pans, 9 x 1½ inches, greased with olive oil if desired.

MEAT TOPPINGS

½ to 1 pound bulk Italian sausage, cooked and drained
1 package (3½ ounces) sliced pepperoni

VEGETABLE TOPPINGS

Sliced mushrooms
Chopped green or red pepper
Chopped onion
Sliced ripe olives
Sliced pimiento-stuffed olives
Coarsely chopped sun-dried tomatoes in oil

Deep-dish Pizza

6 SERVINGS

Deep-dish Crust (below)
Sauce (below)
Meat Toppings (below)
Vegetable Toppings (below)
1½ to 2 cups shredded mozzarella cheese
  (6 to 8 ounces)

Place oven rack in lowest position. Heat oven to 425°. Prepare Deep-dish Crust; spread with Sauce. Top with one of the Meat Toppings and desired Vegetable Toppings. Sprinkle with mozzarella. Bake on lowest oven rack until crust is brown and cheese is melted and bubbly, 15 to 20 minutes.

DEEP-DISH CRUST

1 package active dry yeast
¾ cup warm water (105° to 115°)
3 cups baking mix

Dissolve yeast in water. Stir in baking mix; beat vigorously 20 strokes. Turn dough onto surface generously dusted with baking mix. Knead until smooth and no longer sticky, about 60 times. Let dough rise 5 minutes.

Press dough in bottom and up sides of greased jelly roll pan, 15½ x 10½ x 1 inch. Or pat into rectangle, 13 x 10 inches, on greased cookie sheet; pinch edges of rectangle, forming ¾-inch rim.

SAUCE

1 can (15 ounces) tomato sauce
1 teaspoon dried basil leaves
1 teaspoon dried oregano leaves
1 clove garlic, finely chopped

Mix all ingredients.

MEAT TOPPINGS

½ to 1 pound ground beef, cooked and drained
½ to 1 pound bulk Italian sausage, cooked and drained
1 package (3½ ounces) sliced pepperoni
1 package (6 ounces) sliced Canadian-style bacon

VEGETABLE TOPPINGS

Sliced mushrooms
Chopped green pepper
Sliced green onions or chopped onion
Sliced ripe olives

Bacon and Swiss Cheese Pizza

Crust (below)
10 slices bacon, crisply cooked and crumbled
1½ cups shredded Swiss cheese (6 ounces)
⅓ cup sliced green onions (with tops)
2 eggs
2 tablespoons milk
⅛ teaspoon pepper
2 medium tomatoes, sliced
2 tablespoons grated Parmesan cheese

Heat oven to 400°. Prepare Crust; top with bacon, Swiss cheese and onions.

Beat eggs, milk and pepper with hand beater; pour evenly over top. Top with tomatoes; sprinkle with Parmesan cheese. Sprinkle with snipped parsley if desired. Bake until crust is golden and eggs are set, 20 to 25 minutes.

CRUST

2 cups baking mix
⅓ cup hot water
1 tablespoon vegetable oil

Mix baking mix, water and oil. Turn onto cloth-covered surface dusted with baking mix. Knead 60 times. Roll dough into 12-inch circle. Place in ungreased 12-inch pizza pan.

Vegetable Pizza with Wheat Germ Crust

6 SERVINGS

Wheat Germ Crust (below)
1 cup shredded Monterey Jack cheese (4 ounces)
1 can (8 ounces) pizza sauce
1 small zucchini, thinly sliced
1 cup sliced mushrooms or 1 jar (4.5 ounces)
    sliced mushrooms, drained
3 green onions (with tops), sliced
1 cup shredded Cheddar cheese (4 ounces)

Heat oven to 425°. Prepare Wheat Germ Crust; sprinkle with Monterey Jack cheese. Drizzle with pizza sauce. Arrange zucchini, mushrooms and onions on pizza sauce; sprinkle with Cheddar cheese. Bake until crust is golden brown, about 20 minutes. Garnish with alfalfa sprouts and avocado slices if desired.

WHEAT GERM CRUST

2 cups baking mix
$1/4$ cup wheat germ
$2/3$ cup cold water

Mix baking mix, wheat germ and water until soft dough forms; beat vigorously 20 strokes. Pat dough into 11-inch circle on greased cookie sheet, building up $1/2$-inch edge. Or pat in greased 12-inch pizza pan with floured fingers.

Unbaked Greek-style Pizza

Greek-style Pizza

Crust (below)
1 cup shredded Kasseri or mozzarella cheese
    (4 ounces)
1 package (10 ounces) frozen chopped spinach,
    thawed and squeezed dry
½ pound ground lamb
1 tablespoon snipped fresh oregano leaves or
    1 teaspoon dried oregano leaves
1 medium tomato, chopped
½ cup crumbled feta cheese
½ cup Greek or ripe olives, cut up

Place oven rack in lowest position of oven. Heat oven to 425°. Prepare Crust; sprinkle remaining ingredients evenly over top to within ½ inch of edge. Bake on lowest oven rack until crust is golden brown, 25 to 30 minutes. Drizzle with 1 tablespoon olive oil if desired.

CRUST

1 package active dry yeast
1 cup warm water (105° to 115°)
2½ cups all-purpose flour
2 tablespoons olive or vegetable oil
1 teaspoon sugar
1 teaspoon salt

Dissolve yeast in warm water in 2½-quart bowl. Stir in remaining ingredients; beat vigorously 20 strokes. Let rest 5 minutes.

Press dough in greased 12-inch pizza pan or into 11-inch circle on greased cookie sheet with floured fingers.

Greek-style Pizza

Desserts

Some of these irresistibly easy recipes, such as fudgy Brownies and elegant French Silk Tart, couldn't be more classic. On the innovative side are our very pretty Berry Pirouette and a delicate Apricot Chantilly Torte. The latter is garnished with Chocolate Apricots, which are also wonderful alone with coffee.

Double Cherry Crumble

8 SERVINGS

1 can (21 ounces) cherry pie filling
1 can (about 16 ounces) pitted dark sweet
  cherries, drained
⅔ cup quick-cooking oats
½ cup baking mix
½ cup packed brown sugar
¼ cup chopped nuts, if desired
¼ cup firm margarine or butter
1 teaspoon ground cinnamon

Mix pie filling and cherries in ungreased square pan, 8 x 8 x 2 inches. Mix remaining ingredients until crumbly; sprinkle over fruit.

Bake uncovered in 375° oven until fruit is hot and bubbly and topping is brown, about 45 minutes.

TO MICROWAVE: Mix pie filling and cherries in square microwavable dish, 8 x 8 x 2 inches. Mix remaining ingredients until crumbly; sprinkle over fruit. Microwave uncovered on high (100%) until fruit is hot and bubbly, 7 to 10 minutes. Let stand uncovered 10 minutes.

Double Cherry Crumble

Berry Pirouette

1¾ cups boiling water
2 packages (3 ounces each) raspberry-flavored
  gelatin
1 package (16 ounces) frozen boysenberries,
  partially thawed
2 cups chilled whipping cream
1 package (5½ ounces) tubular-shaped pirouette
  cookies (about 24)

Pour boiling water on gelatin in large bowl; stir until gelatin is dissolved. Reserve 3 to 5 berries for garnish. Place remaining berries in food processor workbowl fitted with steel blade or in blender container. Cover and process until smooth. Stir berries into gelatin. Refrigerate until very thick but not set, about 1 hour.

Beat gelatin mixture on high speed until thick and fluffy, about 4 minutes. Beat 1 cup of the whipping cream in chilled bowl until stiff; fold into gelatin mixture. Pour into springform pan, 9 x 3 inches. Refrigerate until set, about 3 hours.

Run knife around edge of dessert to loosen; remove side of pan. Place dessert on serving plate. Beat remaining whipping cream in chilled bowl until stiff. Spread side of dessert with half of the whipped cream.

Carefully cut cookies crosswise into halves. Arrange cookies, cut sides down, vertically around side of dessert; press lightly. Garnish with remaining whipped cream and berries.

Peach Pirouette: Substitute 1 package (16 ounces) frozen sliced peaches, partially thawed, for the boysenberries and orange-flavored gelatin for the raspberry-flavored gelatin. Reserve 3 peach slices for garnish.

Berry Pirouette

Frozen Cherry Cream

2 cups pitted dark sweet cherries
1/4 cup light corn syrup
3 tablespoons cherry brandy
1 cup chilled whipping cream

Place cherries, corn syrup and brandy in workbowl of food processor fitted with steel blade or in blender container. Cover and process until coarsely chopped. Pour into square pan or baking dish, 9 x 9 x 2 inches. Cover and freeze until partially frozen, about 1 hour.

Beat whipping cream in chilled medium bowl until stiff. Stir cherry mixture; fold into whipped cream. Pour into pan. Cover and freeze, stirring once, until firm, about 2 hours. Let stand 10 minutes.

Frozen Raspberry Yogurt Dessert

Pastry (below)
2 cups chilled whipping cream
1/4 cup powdered sugar
1 container (8 ounces) raspberry yogurt
1 package (10 ounces) frozen raspberries,
    partially thawed

Heat oven to 400°. Prepare Pastry; spread in ungreased rectangular pan, 13 x 9 x 2 inches. Bake until edges are golden, 12 to 15 minutes; cool.

Beat whipping cream and powdered sugar in chilled large bowl until stiff. Fold yogurt and raspberries into whipped cream; spoon over baked pastry. Cover and freeze at least 8 hours. Remove from freezer 20 to 25 minutes before serving.

PASTRY

1 1/2 cups all-purpose flour
1 cup margarine or butter, softened
1/2 cup powdered sugar

Beat all ingredients in large bowl on low speed 1 minute, scraping bowl constantly. Beat on medium speed until creamy, about 2 minutes.

Frozen Pineapple and Orange Yogurt Dessert: Substitute orange yogurt for the raspberry yogurt. Drain 1 can (15 1/2 ounces) crushed pineapple in syrup, reserving 1/4 cup syrup. Substitute pineapple and reserved syrup for the raspberries.

Frozen Strawberry Yogurt Dessert: Substitute strawberry yogurt for the raspberry yogurt and frozen strawberries for the frozen raspberries.

Cherry Ribbon Cake Slices

1 prepared angel food loaf cake (about
  7½ x 4 inches)
1 pint chocolate or French vanilla ice cream,
  slightly softened
1 can (21 ounces) sweet cherry fruit filling
2 tablespoons crème de cassis or kirsch, if desired

Carefully split cake horizontally to make 2 layers. Spread ice cream over bottom layer; place top layer on ice cream. Wrap and freeze until firm, at least 4 hours.

Heat cherry filling until warm; stir in crème de cassis. Cut filled cake into slices. Spoon warm cherry filling over each slice.

Peanut Fudge Ice-cream Dessert

12 SERVINGS

2 cups chocolate wafer crumbs (about 36 wafers)
⅓ cup margarine or butter, melted
¼ cup sugar
1 cup chopped peanuts
½ cup chocolate fudge topping
½ cup caramel-flavored topping
1 half-gallon brick vanilla ice cream
½ cup chocolate fudge topping

Mix wafer crumbs, margarine and sugar. Press firmly in ungreased square pan, 9 x 9 x 2 inches. Mix 1 cup peanuts, ½ cup fudge topping and the caramel-flavored topping. Spread over crumb mixture.

Cut ice cream crosswise into 2-inch slices; place on peanut mixture. Let stand until slightly softened; spread evenly.

Drizzle with ½ cup fudge topping. Cover and freeze until firm, at least 12 hours. Serve with additional chocolate fudge topping and peanuts if desired.

Following pages: Cherry Ribbon Cake Slice (left) and Peanut Fudge Ice-cream Dessert

DESSERTS

Strawberry Sour Cream Pie

Graham Cracker Crust (below)
Strawberry Glacé (below)
1 cup dairy sour cream
1 cup milk
1 package (4 ounces) chocolate instant pudding
    and pie filling
1½ cups sliced strawberries

Bake Graham Cracker Crust; cool. Prepare Strawberry Glacé; cool. Beat sour cream and milk with hand beater until smooth. Mix in pudding and pie filling (dry) until smooth and slightly thickened. Pour into crust.

Arrange strawberries over filling. Pour Strawberry Glacé over strawberries. Refrigerate until firm, about 2 hours. Top with whipped cream if desired.

GRAHAM CRACKER CRUST

1½ cups graham cracker crumbs (about 20
    squares)
3 tablespoons sugar
⅓ cup margarine or butter, melted

Heat oven to 350°. Mix crumbs, sugar and margarine. Press firmly and evenly against bottom and side of ungreased pie plate, 9 x 1¼ inches. Bake 10 minutes.

STRAWBERRY GLACÉ

½ cup sliced strawberries
¼ cup water
½ cup sugar
1 tablespoon plus 1½ teaspoons cornstarch
¼ cup water

Heat strawberries and ¼ cup water to simmering in 1-quart saucepan; simmer uncovered 3 minutes. Mix sugar and cornstarch in small bowl; stir in ¼ cup water. Stir into hot strawberry mixture. Cook, stirring constantly, until mixture thickens and boils. Boil and stir 1 minute.

Apricot Chantilly Torte

1 package (6 ounces) dried apricots
1 can (8 ounces) apricot halves, undrained
2 cups chilled whipping cream
¼ cup powdered sugar
2 tablespoons amaretto or chocolate-flavored
    liqueur, if desired
1 teaspoon vanilla
1 tin (5 ounces) Austrian light dessert wafers
Chocolate Apricots (below) or toasted chopped
    almonds

Reserve 8 to 10 dried apricot halves for Chocolate Apricots if desired. Place remaining dried apricots and the apricot halves in food processor workbowl fitted with steel blade or in blender container. Cover and process until almost smooth. Beat whipping cream, powdered sugar, amaretto and vanilla in chilled bowl until stiff; fold in apricots.

Spread 1 tablespoon whipped cream mixture in 7-inch circle on center of serving plate. Arrange 6 wafers, with points in center, on whipped cream on plate, forming a circle. Carefully spread ¾ cup whipped cream mixture on wafers up to edge of circle. Repeat 5 times, ending with remaining whipped cream mixture.

Carefully cover and refrigerate at least 8 hours but no longer than 36 hours (torte will mellow and become moist). Garnish with Chocolate Apricots and whipped cream if desired.

CHOCOLATE APRICOTS

¼ cup semisweet chocolate chips
1 teaspoon shortening
8 to 10 dried apricot halves

Heat chocolate chips and shortening over low heat, stirring constantly, until melted.

Dip apricot halves ¾ of the way into chocolate mixture; place on flat plate covered with waxed paper. Refrigerate uncovered until chocolate is firm, at least 30 minutes but no longer than 24 hours.

Following pages: Apricot Chantilly Torte

French Silk Tart

1 cup sugar
¾ cup margarine or butter, softened
1½ teaspoons instant coffee
1½ teaspoons vanilla
¼ teaspoon cream of tartar
3 ounces unsweetened chocolate, melted and
   cooled
3 eggs
10-inch baked tart shell or 9-inch baked pie shell
1 cup chilled whipping cream
2 tablespoons powdered sugar

Beat sugar and margarine in small bowl until light and fluffy. Stir in coffee (dry), vanilla, cream of tartar and chocolate. Beat in eggs until light and fluffy, about 3 minutes. Pour into tart shell. Refrigerate until set, 3 to 4 hours. Or cover with plastic wrap and freeze at least 8 hours.

If tart is frozen, remove from freezer 15 minutes before serving. Beat whipping cream and powdered sugar in chilled bowl until stiff. Top tart with whipped cream.

NOTE: For milder chocolate flavor and more pronounced coffee flavor, decrease chocolate to 1 ounce.

Peach Bavarian Cream with Cherries

¾ cup boiling water
1 package (3 ounces) peach-flavored gelatin
1 package (3 ounces) cream cheese, softened
1 cup reconstituted harvest blend fruit juice
   cocktail or white grape juice
1 cup chilled whipping cream
1 can (21 ounces) sweet cherry fruit filling

Pour boiling water on gelatin in large bowl; stir until gelatin is dissolved. Gradually stir 3 tablespoons gelatin mixture into cream cheese until smooth and creamy. Stir cream cheese mixture into gelatin in bowl until well blended; stir in juice. Refrigerate, stirring occasionally, until mixture mounds slightly when dropped from a spoon, about 1 hour.

Beat whipping cream in chilled bowl until stiff. Beat gelatin mixture until foamy, about 1 minute; fold in whipped cream. Pour into 4-cup mold or 6 to 8 small molds. Refrigerate until firm, about 4 hours.

Loosen dessert by dipping mold quickly into warm water; unmold on serving plate or dessert plates. If desired, stir 1 to 2 tablespoons fruit juice into cherry filling until desired consistency; serve with dessert.

Peach Mousse

Raspberry Currant Sauce (page 158)
2 large peaches, peeled and cut up
    (about 2 cups)
1/2 teaspoon grated lemon peel
2 tablespoons lemon juice
1 envelope unflavored gelatin
1 egg white
1/8 teaspoon cream of tartar
1/8 teaspoon salt
1/4 cup sugar
1/2 cup chilled whipping cream

Prepare Raspberry Currant Sauce. Place peaches, lemon peel and lemon juice in food processor workbowl fitted with steel blade or in blender container. Cover and process until smooth.

Pour into 1½-quart saucepan. Sprinkle with gelatin; let stand 1 minute to soften. Heat over low heat, stirring constantly, until gelatin is dissolved. Remove from heat; place saucepan in bowl of ice and water or refrigerate, stirring occasionally, until mixture mounds slightly when dropped from a spoon, about 15 minutes.

Beat egg white, cream of tartar and salt in medium bowl until foamy. Beat in sugar, 1 tablespoon at a time; continue beating until stiff and glossy. Fold in peach mixture.

Beat whipping cream in chilled bowl until stiff; fold into peach mixture. Cover and refrigerate at least 2 hours but no longer than 24 hours.

Spoon into dessert dishes; serve with sauce. Garnish with additional fresh fruit if desired. Refrigerate any remaining dessert.

Hawaiian Ice-cream Dessert

1 can (20 ounces) crushed pineapple in syrup
1 package (13¾ ounces) soft coconut macaroons
1 half-gallon vanilla ice cream, softened
½ cup toasted chopped macadamia nuts or
  almonds
Whipped cream

Heat oven to 400°. Drain pineapple, reserving ¼ cup syrup. Crumble macaroons into ungreased jelly roll pan, 15½ x 10½ x 1 inch. Bake uncovered, stirring occasionally, until golden brown, 8 to 10 minutes; cool completely.

Reserve 2 tablespoons macaroon crumbs. Mix remaining crumbs and the pineapple syrup in ungreased springform pan, 9 x 3 inches; press evenly on bottom and 1 inch up side of pan. Mix ice cream, nuts and pineapple; spread in pan. Cover and freeze until firm, at least 8 hours.

Run knife around edge of dessert to loosen; remove side of pan. Spoon or pipe whipped cream on top of dessert; sprinkle with reserved macaroon crumbs.

Hawaiian Ice-cream Dessert

Citrus Ice-cream Cake

1 package (18.25 ounces) lemon cake mix
   with pudding
½ cup chilled whipping cream
1 quart orange sherbet, softened
1 quart vanilla ice cream, softened
Whipped cream
Fruit

Bake cake in 2 round pans, 9 x 1½ inches, as directed on package; cool completely. Split 1 layer horizontally to make 2 layers. (Use remaining layer as desired.) Place 1 split layer, cut side up, in ungreased springform pan, 9 x 3 inches.

Beat whipping cream in chilled large bowl until stiff; fold in sherbet. Spoon sherbet mixture and ice cream alternately into pan. Carefully cut through mixture and ice cream with spoon or metal spatula several times for marbled effect; spread evenly.

Cut remaining split layer into 12 wedges. Arrange 11 of the wedges, cut sides up and rounded edges touching side of pan, on ice cream. (Use remaining wedge as desired.) Cover and freeze until firm.

Remove from freezer and refrigerate 30 minutes before serving. Run knife around edge of dessert to loosen; remove side of pan. Garnish with whipped cream and fruit.

FIX IT AND FORGET IT

288

Apricot-Banana Bars

¾ cup packed brown sugar
½ cup margarine or butter, softened
1 jar (12 ounces) apricot preserves
1 teaspoon vanilla
2 eggs
2 cups all-purpose flour
¾ cup mashed bananas (about 2 medium)
½ cup chopped pecans
1 teaspoon baking powder
½ teaspoon baking soda
¼ teaspoon salt
Apricot Glaze (below)

Heat oven to 350°. Mix brown sugar and margarine in large bowl. Reserve 2 tablespoons of the preserves for Apricot Glaze. Stir remaining preserves, the vanilla and eggs into brown sugar mixture.

Stir in remaining ingredients except Apricot Glaze; mix until dry ingredients are moistened. Spread in greased and floured jelly roll pan, 15½ x 10½ x 1 inch. Bake until golden brown, about 30 minutes. Spread with Apricot Glaze while warm; cool. Cut into 3 x 1-inch bars.

APRICOT GLAZE

1½ cups powdered sugar
2 tablespoons reserved apricot preserves
1 tablespoon water

Mix all ingredients until desired consistency.

Chocolate Nut Squares

1 cup packed brown sugar
1 cup margarine or butter, softened
1½ teaspoons vanilla
1 egg
2 cups all-purpose flour
½ cup light corn syrup
2 tablespoons margarine or butter
1 package (12 ounces) semisweet chocolate chips
1 can (12 ounces) salted mixed nuts

Heat oven to 350°. Mix brown sugar, 1 cup margarine, the vanilla and egg in large bowl. Stir in flour. Spread evenly in bottom of ungreased rectangular pan, 13 x 9 x 2 inches. Bake until light brown, 20 to 22 minutes. Cool 20 minutes.

Heat corn syrup, 2 tablespoons margarine and the chocolate chips over low heat, stirring constantly, until chips are melted. Cool 20 minutes.

Spread chocolate mixture over layer in pan. Sprinkle with nuts; gently press into chocolate. Refrigerate uncovered until chocolate is firm, about 2 hours. Cut into 1½-inch squares.

Following pages: Chocolate Nut Squares (left) and Marbled Brownies

Marbled Brownies

Cream Cheese Filling (below)
1 cup margarine or butter
4 ounces unsweetened chocolate
2 cups sugar
2 teaspoons vanilla
4 eggs
1½ cups all-purpose flour
½ teaspoon salt
1 cup coarsely chopped nuts

Heat oven to 350°. Prepare Cream Cheese Filling. Heat margarine and chocolate over low heat, stirring occasionally, until melted; cool. Beat chocolate mixture, sugar, vanilla and eggs in large bowl on medium speed 1 minute, scraping bowl occasionally. Beat in flour and salt on low speed 30 seconds, scraping bowl occasionally. Beat on medium speed 1 minute; stir in nuts.

Spread half of the batter in greased square pan, 9 x 9 x 2 inches; spread with Cream Cheese Filling. Gently spread remaining batter over filling. Gently swirl through batter with spoon in an over-and-under motion for marbled effect.

Bake until wooden pick inserted in center comes out clean, 55 to 65 minutes; cool. Cut into 1½ x 1-inch bars.

CREAM CHEESE FILLING

1 package (8 ounces) cream cheese, softened
¼ cup sugar
1 teaspoon ground cinnamon
1½ teaspoons vanilla
1 egg

Beat all ingredients 2 minutes, scraping bowl occasionally.

Brownies

½ cup margarine or butter
1 package (12 ounces) semisweet chocolate chips
1⅔ cups sugar
1¼ cups all-purpose or whole wheat flour
1 teaspoon vanilla
½ teaspoon baking powder
½ teaspoon salt
3 eggs

Heat oven to 350°. Heat margarine and chocolate chips in 3-quart saucepan over low heat, stirring constantly, until melted. Beat in remaining ingredients until smooth; stir in 1 cup chopped nuts if desired. Spread in greased rectangular pan, 13 x 9 x 2 inches. Bake until center is set, about 30 minutes; cool completely. Cut into 2 x 1½-inch bars. Store tightly covered.

Zucchini and Raisin Bars

1¼ cups packed brown sugar
½ cup margarine or butter, softened
1 teaspoon vanilla
2 eggs
2 cups whole wheat flour
2 teaspoons baking soda
¾ teaspoon ground cinnamon
½ teaspoon ground nutmeg
¼ teaspoon ground cloves
1½ cups shredded zucchini
1 cup golden raisins
Lemon Glaze or Cream Cheese Frosting (below)

Heat oven to 350°. Mix brown sugar, margarine, vanilla and eggs in large bowl. Stir in flour, baking soda, cinnamon, nutmeg and cloves; stir in zucchini and raisins. Spread in greased rectangular pan, 13 x 9 x 2 inches.

Bake until wooden pick inserted in center comes out clean, 25 to 35 minutes. Spread with Lemon Glaze while warm, or cool and frost with Cream Cheese Frosting. Cut into 2 x 1½-inch bars. Refrigerate any remaining bars.

LEMON GLAZE

1½ cups powdered sugar
2 tablespoons margarine or butter, softened
1 to 2 tablespoons lemon juice

Mix sugar and margarine. Stir in lemon juice, 1 teaspoon at a time, until smooth and of desired consistency.

CREAM CHEESE FROSTING

1 package (3 ounces) cream cheese, softened
¼ cup plus 2 tablespoons margarine or butter, softened
1 teaspoon vanilla
2 cups powdered sugar

Mix cream cheese, margarine and vanilla in medium bowl. Gradually beat in powdered sugar until smooth and of spreading consistency.

Applesauce Snack Cake

1²/₃ cups all-purpose flour
1 cup packed brown sugar
1¹/₂ teaspoons ground allspice
1 teaspoon baking soda
¹/₂ teaspoon salt
¹/₂ cup applesauce
¹/₃ cup chopped nuts
¹/₂ cup water
¹/₃ cup vegetable oil
1 teaspoon vinegar
Apple Cider Sauce (below)

Heat oven to 350°. Mix flour, brown sugar, allspice, baking soda and salt with fork in ungreased square pan, 8 x 8 x 2 inches. Mix in remaining ingredients. Bake until wooden pick inserted in center comes out clean, 35 to 40 minutes. Prepare Apple Cider Sauce; serve with warm cake.

APPLE CIDER SAUCE

¹/₂ cup packed brown sugar
¹/₄ cup margarine or butter
¹/₄ cup apple cider or orange juice
2 tablespoons whipping cream

Heat all ingredients to rolling boil in heavy 1¹/₂-quart saucepan over high heat, stirring constantly; reduce heat slightly. Boil 3 minutes, stirring frequently. (Watch carefully; mixture burns easily.) Refrigerate any remaining sauce.

TO MICROWAVE: For cake, mix as directed in ungreased round microwavable dish, 8 x 1¹/₂ inches. Place dish on inverted microwavable pie plate, 9 x 1¹/₄ inches, in microwave oven. Microwave uncovered on medium (50%), rotating dish ¹/₄ turn every 5 minutes, until top springs back when touched lightly, 15 to 17 minutes. (Center top may appear moist but will continue to cook while standing.) Let stand uncovered on flat heatproof surface (do not let stand on wire rack).

For sauce, decrease apple cider to 2 tablespoons. Place all ingredients in 4-cup microwavable measure. Microwave uncovered on high (100%) just to boiling, 1¹/₂ to 2 minutes; stir. Microwave uncovered, stirring every minute, until thickened, 2 to 3 minutes longer.

Applesauce Snack Cake

Hot Fudge Sundae Cake

1 cup all-purpose flour
¾ cup granulated sugar
2 tablespoons cocoa
2 teaspoons baking powder
¼ teaspoon salt
½ cup milk
2 tablespoons vegetable oil
1 teaspoon vanilla
1 cup chopped nuts, if desired
1 cup packed brown sugar
¼ cup cocoa
1¾ cups hottest tap water
Ice cream

Heat oven to 350°. Mix flour, granulated sugar, 2 tablespoons cocoa, the baking powder and salt in ungreased square pan, 9 x 9 x 2 inches. Mix in milk, oil and vanilla with fork until smooth. Stir in nuts. Spread in pan. Sprinkle with brown sugar and ¼ cup cocoa. Pour hot water over batter.

Bake uncovered 40 minutes. While warm, spoon into dessert dishes and top with ice cream. Spoon sauce from pan onto each serving.

Butterscotch Sundae Cake: Substitute 1 package (6 ounces) butterscotch chips for the nuts. Decrease brown sugar to ½ cup and the ¼ cup cocoa to 2 tablespoons.

Marshmallow Sundae Cake: Substitute 1 cup miniature marshmallows for the nuts.

Peanut Sundae Cake: Substitute ½ cup peanut butter and ½ cup chopped peanuts for the nuts.

Raisin Sundae Cake: Substitute 1 cup raisins for the nuts.

TO MICROWAVE: Mix flour, granulated sugar, 2 tablespoons cocoa, the baking powder and salt in 2-quart microwavable casserole. Stir in milk, oil and vanilla with fork until smooth. Stir in nuts. Sprinkle with brown sugar and ¼ cup cocoa. Pour hot water over batter.

Microwave uncovered on medium (50%) 9 minutes; rotate casserole ¼ turn. Microwave uncovered on high (100%) until top is almost dry, 5 to 7 minutes longer. Serve as directed above.

Chocolate Chip Date Cake

⅔ cup hot water
½ cup cut-up dates
½ teaspoon baking soda
⅓ cup vegetable oil
1 egg
1 cup all-purpose flour
½ cup semisweet miniature chocolate chips
¼ cup granulated sugar
¼ cup packed brown sugar
½ teaspoon baking soda
½ teaspoon vanilla
¼ teaspoon salt
Nut Chocolate Chip Topping (below)

NUT CHOCOLATE CHIP TOPPING

½ cup chopped nuts
½ cup semisweet miniature chocolate chips
2 tablespoons packed brown sugar

Heat oven to 350°. Pour hot water over dates in medium bowl; stir in ½ teaspoon baking soda. Let stand 5 minutes.

Stir remaining ingredients except Nut Chocolate Chip Topping into date mixture. Pour into ungreased square pan, 8 x 8 x 2 inches; sprinkle with topping. Bake until wooden pick inserted in center comes out clean, about 35 minutes.

Mix all ingredients.

TO MICROWAVE: Pour batter into ungreased round microwavable dish, 8 x 1½ inches; sprinkle with Nut Chocolate Chip Topping. Place dish on inverted microwavable dinner plate in microwave oven.

Microwave uncovered on medium (50%) 3 minutes; rotate dish ½ turn. Microwave uncovered 3 minutes longer; rotate dish ½ turn. Microwave uncovered on high (100%) 2 minutes; rotate dish ½ turn. Microwave uncovered until wooden pick inserted in center comes out clean, 1½ to 2½ minutes longer. (Parts of surface may appear wet but will continue to cook while standing.) Let stand uncovered on flat heatproof surface 10 minutes (do not let stand on wire rack); cool on wire rack.

Apple Cider Crisp

8 cups sliced pared all-purpose apples (about
    8 medium)
½ cup raisins
¾ cup apple cider
1 cup graham cracker crumbs (about
    12 crackers)
½ cup packed brown sugar
1 teaspoon ground cinnamon
¼ teaspoon ground nutmeg
¼ cup plus 2 tablespoons margarine or butter,
    melted

Heat oven to 350°. Arrange apples and raisins in ungreased rectangular baking dish, 11 x 7 x 1½ inches. Pour cider over apples and raisins. Mix cracker crumbs, brown sugar, cinnamon and nutmeg; stir in margarine thoroughly. Sprinkle evenly over apples and raisins.

Bake until apples are tender, 50 to 55 minutes. Serve warm; top with ice cream or Apple Cider Sauce (page 295) if desired.

Walnut Torte

1½ cups chopped walnuts
1½ cups vanilla wafer crumbs (about
    33 wafers)
1 cup packed brown sugar
1 cup margarine or butter, melted
1 package (18.25 ounces) devil's food cake mix
    with pudding
1½ cups chilled whipping cream
3 tablespoons granulated sugar
1 teaspoon vanilla

Heat oven to 350°. Mix walnuts, wafer crumbs, brown sugar and margarine. Spread ¾ cup mixture in each of 2 ungreased round pans, 9 x 1½ inches; reserve remaining walnut mixture. Prepare cake mix as directed on package. Pour 1¼ cups batter over walnut mixture in each pan; refrigerate remaining batter.

Bake until tops spring back when touched lightly, about 20 minutes. Immediately remove from pans; invert. Repeat with remaining walnut mixture and batter. Cool layers completely.

Beat whipping cream, granulated sugar and vanilla in chilled bowl until stiff.

Place 1 layer, walnut side up, on serving plate; spread with ¾ cup whipped cream. Repeat with remaining layers and whipped cream; refrigerate until chilled.

Peach and Blueberry Cobbler

3 cups sliced peaches (5 or 6 medium)
2 cups blueberries
2 tablespoons lemon juice
⅔ cup sugar
3 tablespoons all-purpose flour
½ teaspoon ground cinnamon
2 tablespoons margarine or butter
1 cup all-purpose flour
2 tablespoons sugar
1½ teaspoons baking powder
¼ teaspoon salt
⅓ cup shortening
3 tablespoons milk
1 egg

Heat oven to 375°. Arrange peaches and blueberries in ungreased square baking dish, 8 x 8 x 2 inches; sprinkle with lemon juice. Mix ⅔ cup sugar, 3 tablespoons flour and the cinnamon; sprinkle over fruit. Dot with margarine.

Mix 1 cup flour, 2 tablespoons sugar, the baking powder and salt; cut in shortening until mixture resembles fine crumbs. Mix in milk and egg. Drop dough by 9 spoonfuls onto fruit mixture. Bake uncovered until topping is golden brown, 25 to 30 minutes. Serve warm with cream or ice cream if desired.

Peach-Pecan Tart

Butter Crust (below)
Orange Glaze (below)
2 packages (3 ounces each) cream cheese, softened
4 cups sliced peaches (about 4 medium)
½ cup chopped pecans

Bake Butter Crust; cool. Prepare Orange Glaze. Beat cream cheese until smooth; spread on bottom of crust.

Arrange peaches on crust; sprinkle with pecans. Spoon Orange Glaze over top. Refrigerate until set, about 2 hours.

BUTTER CRUST

1⅓ cups all-purpose flour
⅓ cup packed brown sugar
⅔ cup margarine or butter, softened

Heat oven to 400°. Mix flour and brown sugar; cut in margarine until crumbly. Press firmly and evenly against bottom and side of ungreased 12-inch pizza pan. Bake until light brown, 10 to 15 minutes.

ORANGE GLAZE

1 cup sugar
3 tablespoons cornstarch
¼ teaspoon salt
1 cup orange juice
½ cup water

Mix sugar, cornstarch and salt in 1-quart saucepan. Gradually stir in orange juice and water. Heat to boiling over medium heat, stirring constantly. Boil and stir 1 minute; cool.

Brown Sugar Pear Tart

Pecan Crust (below)
3 or 4 medium pears (about 2 pounds), pared
½ cup packed brown sugar
1 tablespoon all-purpose flour
½ teaspoon ground cinnamon
1 tablespoon margarine or butter

Bake Pecan Crust. Cut each pear lengthwise into halves; remove core. Place each pear half, cut side down, on cutting surface. Cut crosswise into thin slices. With spatula, lift each pear half and arrange on crust, separating and overlapping slices (retain pear shape) to cover surface of crust.

Mix brown sugar, flour, cinnamon and margarine; sprinkle over pears. Bake in 375° oven until crust is golden brown and pears are tender, 15 to 20 minutes.

PECAN CRUST

1⅓ cups all-purpose flour
⅓ cup packed brown sugar
⅓ cup finely chopped pecans
½ teaspoon ground nutmeg
½ teaspoon grated lemon peel
⅔ cup margarine or butter, softened

Heat oven to 375°. Mix all ingredients except margarine; cut in margarine until crumbly. Press firmly and evenly against bottom and side of ungreased 12-inch pizza pan. Bake 8 minutes.

Brown Sugar Pear Tart

Index

M indicates microwave
instructions included

M indicates microwave
instructions included

M indicates microwave
instructions included

M indicates microwave
instructions included

M indicates microwave
instructions included

Credits
GENERAL MILLS, INC.

Editor: Kay Emel-Powell
Test Kitchen Home Economists: Mary Hallin Johnson, Mary Jane Friedhoff
Copy Editor: Lauren Long
Editorial Assistant: Anne Oslund
Food Stylists: Cindy Lund, Carol Grones
Photographer: Nanci E. Doonan
Photography Assistant: Carolyn Luxmoore
Director, Betty Crocker Food and Publications Center: Marcia Copeland
Manager: Barbara Jo Davis
Assistant Manager, Publications: Lois Tlusty

PRENTICE HALL PRESS

Creative Director: J. C. Suarès
Designers: Laurence Alexander, Patricia Fabricant, Suzanne Reisel
Prop Stylist: Gail Bailey